THE BATTLE FOR ANCIENT INDIA

THE BATTLE FOR ANCIENT INDIA

An Essay in the Sociopolitics of Indian Archaeology

Dilip K. Chakrabarti

ARYAN BOOKS INTERNATIONAL
New Delhi

THE BATTLE FOR ANCIENT INDIA

ISBN-10: 81-7305-341-3
ISBN-13: 978-81-7305-341-2

First Published in **2008** by:
ARYAN BOOKS INTERNATIONAL
Pooja Apartments, 4B, Ansari Road, New Delhi - 110 002 (India)
Tel.: 23287589, 23255799; Fax: 91-11-23270385
E-mail: aryanbooks@vsnl.com

Computer Typeset and Printed in India at
ABI Prints & Publishing Co., New Delhi.

To
my wife, Sima,
and my daughter,
Nayana (Sonai)

Preface and Acknowledgements

This volume is rooted in my *Colonial Indology: Sociopolitics of the Ancient Indian Past* (1997) and demonstrates in the context of Indian archaeology how the grip of "colonial Indology" is still an intellectual force cutting across the national boundaries. Among the archaeologists at least this trend of thought has been more visible in the post-1947 period than in the period preceding it. This book also shows how the various current debates regarding Indian archaeology and ancient history end up by being an issue of "progress versus reaction" or "secularism versus communalism" and how such assertions are only a reflection of the political expediency of the concerned scholars.

In its quest to underline the various sociopolitical subtexts of opinions in the field of modern Indian archaeology, the book clearly focuses on how these opinions have taken birth and evolved and what exactly is their academic basis. Unless we are aware of the socio-political ramifications of our archaeological opinions, it is unlikely that we shall be able to form our own conclusions about them.

This book was written in September-December of 2006, and I am deeply thankful to Dr. Rakesh Tewari and Professor Nayanjot Lahiri for kindly going through the manuscript and offering suggestions. The responsibility of all shortcomings rests with me. I am especially indebted to my colleague Dr. Cameron Petrie who kindly procured for me a copy of S.K. Chatterji's *Modern Review* article. It is dedicated to my wife and daughter, both of whom have always striven hard to make my academic life smooth and even. My daughter also took upon herself the duty of taking down my field dictations and doing photography in the field.

Contents

1

Introduction

I. THE THEME

One is aware that there has been a long-drawn battle to define the core points of our image of ancient India, and one is also aware that this battle is not academic any more and that it is being currently fought with the bitterness and ferocity of interfaith clashes.[1] The internet has long been full of sites which peddle opinions on a wide range of themes related to Indian history, but interestingly, most of them relate to what is abbreviated as AIT (Aryan Invasion Theory) or AMT (Aryan Migration Theory). An inordinate amount of literature is being bandied about on this theme in the internet, testifying to an almost neurotic fascination for a historical premise which I have elsewhere argued to be racist and bereft of any archaeological and historical reality.[2] Another recurrent theme is a generally explicit concern with the need to highlight the multitude of positive aspects of ancient India including its contribution to the sum-total of human knowledge and influence on other cultures. A large part of this discussion seems to be centred around the Vedas.[3]

A third refrain is a strong sense of dissatisfaction with the way the ancient Indian past has been viewed so far. One also detects a sense of bewilderment about it. Why should the dominant academic discourse on ancient India be keen on its portraying it in a poor light – hardly original and invariably late in the progression of human cultural development? In recent years this sense of bewilderment has found clear expression in the writings of Rajiv Malhotra who has questioned in no uncertain terms the power-structure and the academic rules of the Indian studies establishment of the United States where he lives.[4] In fact, if the websites are any indication, much of this dissatisfaction with the hitherto cherished notions of Indology springs from expatriates like him.

At the other end of the spectrum lies the voice of the politically and otherwise dominant academic establishment of both India and the West, relegating everything that is being said against its cherished premises to the often undefined framework of Hindu fundamentalism or what has come to be known, quite illogically, as *Hindutva* which simply means the essence of being a Hindu and has been used as such by many secular Indian nationalists including Bankim Chandra Chattopadhyay and Rabindra Nath Tagore. On one level, this establishment harps on some incidents like the demolition of a sixteenth century mosque at Ayodhya or the vandalism at the Bhandarkar Oriental Research Institute of Pune, in protest against this institute's supposed support to a Canadian/American author who reputedly made derogatory comments on Sivaji's parentage, and never tires of crying out loud against the real or imagined dilution of secularism in school textbooks, whether in India or in California.[5] On a different level, it tries to deny, or pour scorn on, any evidence that may imply that India in the ancient context was something more than a mere peripheral area in relation to the contemporary centres of civilization in the sphere of scientific and technological developments.[6]

What matters most in all these questionings and the rejoinders they draw, is the fact of questioning itself. That the basic structure of ancient Indian studies is being subjected to close examinations is something that promises well for the discipline. The paradigms we have lived with so far in this field are in many cases built on negligible and often shadowy evidence, combined with large dollops of academic bigotry of various kinds. That this questioning of the framework of the ancient Indian past has also begun to emanate from people, many of whom are not professional students of ancient India but represent a wide range of scientific professions, is singularly heartening. That the concerned academic establishment should react in the way it does, i.e., by associating all such questionings with Hindu fundamentalism, is not possibly a matter of surprise to those who know at the grassroots level how the Indian historical power structure and its international linkages operate. What is a matter of surprise is that a large number of highly educated and professional Indians who have spread around the world in search of livelihood should be so concerned with knowing their ancient past in a way which satisfies their sense of logic, and pride in their roots in an old and distinct civilization.

The present volume is set in this context. *By studying the socio-political implications of some of the current assumptions of Indian archaeology and by noting their associations with different scholars and scholarly groups, it demonstrates that even the apparently remote conclusions about India's prehistoric, proto-historic and early historic past have sub-texts of various kinds and that all these sub-texts have different socio-political implications and agendas.*

II. THE AUTHOR'S OWN APPROACH AND BELIEFS

I must begin by outlining my own position in this chain of archaeology-related politics.

As we all know, the invasion hypotheses of various kinds have long dominated the study of ancient India, with the AIT forming its main cornerstone. In the context of the historical period this has been strengthened by the documented cases of invasions by the Achaemenids, Alexander, Indo-Greeks, Indo-Scythians, Indo-Parthians, Kushans and the Sassanids. A review of the various AIT theories current in Indian archaeology in the 1960s convinced me that these theories were mutually contradictory and based on a series of unsubstantiated beliefs and assertions (Chakrabarti 1968). Later, an examination of the hypothesis that the beginning of iron was related to the coming of the Aryans in India showed that all the evidence, if viewed without commitment to the AIT, pointed to India being an early and independent centre of origin of iron technology (Chakrabarti 1976). In about the same time (Chakrabarti 1977) I undertook an examination of the geographical parameters of all the documented cases of 'invasions' in ancient India. The two main points that I emphasized in this context are that the southern part of central Asia, the eastern rim of Iran, the whole of Afghanistan and the whole of the Indus Valley including the adjacent tract of Kashmir constituted a single political and economic interaction zone throughout Indian history, and that all these cases of 'invasions' took place only after the invading powers consolidated themselves first to the south of the Hindukush which in fact marked the natural northern limits of the Indian subcontinent west of the Himalayas and allied ranges. The implication of this analysis was that these 'invasions' sprang from an area which was within the geographical orbit of the subcontinent itself. Further, while examining the central philosophical assumption behind all the invasion hypotheses or diffusionary hypotheses of Indian archaeology, I realized that these were deeply rooted in the dominant conceptual framework of the ancient Indian past which visualized history as an interplay of race, language and culture (Chakrabarti 1988: 28-33). In 1997 I published a detailed historical study of the concept of race and the racial classificatory studies in the context of Indian population, demonstrating how they coloured the entire scheme of ancient Indian historical studies. The preface of this book introduced its basic theme:

> This book explores some underlying theoretical premises of the Western study of ancient India. These premises developed in response to the colonial need to manipulate the Indians' perception of their past. The need was felt most strongly from the middle of the nineteenth century onwards, and an elaborate racist framework, in which the interrelationship between race, language and culture was a key element, slowly emerged as an explanation of the ancient Indian historical universe. The measure of its success is obvious from the fact that the Indian nationalist historians left this framework unchallenged, preferring to dispute it only in some comparatively minor matters of detail. This book argues that this framework is still in place, and implicitly accepted not merely by Western Indologists but also by their Indian counterparts. The image of the ancient Indian past remains the same. The persistence of the old image is reflective of India's relationship as a part of the Third World with the West and Western historical scholarship.
>
> This book has a further argument. Mere dismantling of the current racist structure of our perception of ancient India and all that it implies will not lead by itself to an Indian perception of the ancient Indian past. Besides, any alternative sense of this past should be something in which all Indians, irrespective of their individual affiliations, can feel having a share. Among other things, the book underlines the total inadequacy of ancient Indian texts to offer fine resolution historical images in chronological and geographical order, and argues that this goal is unlikely to

> be achieved by combining our ahistorical texts with social science theories. This can be achieved only through detailed grassroots investigations of the ancient history of the land and its interrelations with human beings (Chakrabarti 1997: ix).

An outline of the main argument of this book along with an emphasis on "the need of a different past in modern India" was also published in 2000 (Chakrabarti 2000).

> It is only by focusing on the grassroots archaeological investigation, of how communities have adapted themselves to the Indian landscape, that we can escape the bondage of a textual, racist and casteist past (Chakrabarti 2000: 870).

It was also pointed out in this publication that there are differences in how the Indian archaeologists and historians of different socio-economic, educational and institutional backgrounds view the Indian past, with a clear rift emerging between those who feel more at home in English than in their native language and literature and are consequently isolated from their own literary and cultural heritage, and those who were taught in their mother-tongues and find themselves disadvantaged in relation to their 'Westernised' brethren.

In 2003 I tried to define the basic scope of 'nationalist archaeology' in India. In this context I wrote the following:

> It has been far from my intention to try to isolate all the areas and approaches of such a nationalist enquiry. I have only tried to highlight some themes, in the enunciation of which I have been personally involved. What I have tried to do, however, is to argue that the pursuit of a nationalist goal in archaeology is entirely justified as long as this does not bend archaeological data and is not used as an intellectual support for chauvinism. Further, in such multi-ethnic nation-states as India the notion of the ancient past should not be based on the perceived and historically evolving and changing ethnic, linguistic and other differences but on the story of their interconnections and common achievements. A positive archaeological attitude to these achievements is both necessary and justified (Chakrabarti 2003: 279).

The foregoing is meant to explain my role in the debate regarding the socio-political aspects of Indian archaeological studies. It clearly defines my approach and point of view in this field. Countries like India, which have a long history of archaeological research, have identified, in the course of this history, their own professional concerns and methods which in totality constitutes their national traditions of archaeology. It is also my belief that these national traditions deserve every consideration from the archaeologists who do not belong to that tradition and yet find themselves interested in doing archaeological research in those countries.

Going beyond the national archaeological traditions, I find a clear distinction between the First and Third World archaeologies, with the Third World archaeology having a number of common and interrelated denominators. The archaeological notion of the past in these countries was imposed from above by their colonial governments. During the phase of nationalist movements in these countries, there was no special quest by their elite to know the land in terms of its archaeological remains. It also remains true that the number of archaeologists of various colonial countries was always limited and thus they could not play a major role in the emergence of a sense of the archaeological past in these countries, nor were they successful in making archaeology a part of these countries' mainstream historical education. In India, for instance, I have laid the responsibility of evolving a race and language-based approach to the past cultures of India not at the door of the archaeologists but at the door of the sundry 'Indologists' both in and out of the colonial government.

The old framework persists even in the post-colonial context. Archaeology is still not a major part of their mainstream education nor does archaeology play a major role in the identity-formation in most of the Third World countries. The startling discoveries like the one made at Mohenjodaro and Harappa in the early 1920s had certainly played a role in the identity-formation of the Indians, but the general national pride in them seldom went beyond the planning of these cities and their sewage system.

There is still no concept of 'rescue-archaeology' in these areas and their archaeological literature is published overwhelmingly not in the native languages but in English or other Western languages with which most of the people of these countries are unfamiliar. Further, I argued:

> An issue of considerable theoretical interest to these multi-ethnic states of the Third World is to develop a non-sectarian image of

> their past in which their current ethnic groups are not related to a superior/inferior hierarchy. This may turn out to be the most important future task of Third World archaeology (Chakrabarti 2003: 215).

I also believe that the archaeologists do not belong to a single social or intellectual category. It has been necessary to put some stress on this common-sense belief; occasionally archaeologists forget this:

> Western academics themselves could be characterized as a highly mobile, rootless group (often by virtue of occupation), who are on the whole analytical and somewhat detached from politics, despite their leftist leanings (Meskell 2002: 280).

As I shall demonstrate later in the Indian context, such definitions of Western or any other academic group only serve to hide the gross realities of the study of socio-politics of archaeology. It also has the sub-text of hinting that the academics from beyond the West are on the whole not analytical. One is not unduly worried about this sub-text because Meskell is unlikely to be alone in hinting at this; we have come across writings of other American archaeologists who talk of Western archaeologists and the West vis-à-vis Indian archaeologists and India, exactly in this fashion.

This brings me to the question of 'subservience to colonial archaeology' on the part of the Third World archaeologists. This accusation against Third World archaeologists, of whom the present author is one, has been made by M. Vidale (2000), an Italian archaeologist, mainly to defend another Italian archaeologist's (M. Tosi) opinion that the Indus civilization had its origin due to an external impetus. As far as this particular academic opinion is concerned, it was not the opinion of colonial archaeologists who discovered and studied this civilization. They, in fact, thought that the Indus civilization was deeply rooted in the Indian soil. Secondly, I would say that the Western archaeologists of the recent period – and I am familiar with the opinions of those who work in modern India – are usually so aware of their superiority in relation to the natives that self-respecting Indian archaeologists are occasionally forced to wonder if there can ever be a common ground between them. Those of us who are professionally aware of what the colonial archaeologists did in India and know that they and their Indian colleagues laid the foundations of the national tradition of archaeology in the country together, do not really enjoy the spectacle of arrows being thrown at them by people under the umbrella of post-colonial theories of one kind or another. Vidale's critique was also partly directed at Wheeler who did not pursue his find of a pre-Harappan stratum at Harappa where his American successors there both expanded and amplified the archaeological sequence of the site. Wheeler could work in India for mainly three seasons – out of his four years in India, one year was basically wasted because of the disturbances of Partition. He worked for only one season at Harappa. To compare the results of only one season's work with the fruits of almost 20 years' work at the site is possibly an unwarranted and unacceptable exercise.[7]

Is Indian archaeology more political than the archaeology practised in other countries? It is unlikely to be the case. The relationship between archaeology and politics has been pointed out in the case of many countries, and one has only to go through any journal devoted to Biblical archaeology to realize that the concern of many archaeologists working in the Biblical lands is to relate their work to the various groups of people mentioned in the Bible (cf. Dever 1998). As N.A. Silberman comments,

> ... the ideological rationale of American Biblical Archaeology has always been primarily connected with the construction and elaboration of a modern ecumenical consciousness. With participants drawn from a wide range of American seminaries and university departments of religion its emphasis has long been on the study of civilizations and sites directly relevant to the shared appreciation of the Bible and the early history of Judaism and Christianity ... American Biblical Archaeology was ... linked from its earliest days to the American missionary movement which was, before 1856, the sole organized American presence in the Levant (Silberman 1998: 178-179).

This focus on the Bible as the yardstick of judging archaeological finds is, as far as I know, never attributed to any shade of fundamentalism among the Christians, whereas to focus on the Hindu epics in any Indian archaeological enterprise or to think in terms of independent cultural developments in India is to run the risk of being labelled as a Hindu fundamentalist.

In a work of this kind it is always advisable to spell out the personal standpoint of the author. I believe that the history of ancient India has to be judged primarily in its own terms and that there should not be any theory of externally inspired diffusion to explain its cultural development unless there is a strong supportive evidence and unless the hypothesis can be justified in clear geographical terms. As an archaeologist and as an Indian I do not feel any compulsion to explain the history of ancient Indian cultural development as that of a continuous process of 'colonization'.

III. THE IDEA OF INDIA AS A COLONIZED LAND THROUGHOUT HISTORY

This is a term which, in fact, has been used by two noted Indian pre-historians to describe India's prehistoric cultural process. H.D. Sankalia discussed the issue in 1973 and V.N. Misra in 2001. While writing for the major international journal *World Archaeology*, Sankalia wrote:

> ... it would be advisable on present evidence to interpret the principal changes in the development of Indian prehistoric culture as due to small groups of foreigners who, at different times, seem to have entered India from Iran through Afghanistan and Baluchistan ... (Sankalia 1973: 90).

He added that there were scholars who would recommend "to look under our feet and not beyond" and that "older views about invasions and colonizations" were no longer fashionable. In this connection he cites Grahame Clark's article "the invasion hypothesis in British archaeology" in *Antiquity* 40 (1966): 172-189. He, however, found no reason to change his position.

Misra (2001) also does not hesitate to use the term 'colonization' while reviewing the subcontinent's archaeological sequence, and hardly underlines the possibility of an indigenously evolving multi-lineal scenario.

Why the term 'colonization', which implies that India was always a backwater in terms of human progress, should be used to describe India's prehistoric cultural development by two 'Directors' of an Indian institute for archaeological study and research is not clear except that both of them, although at a time-gap of more than twenty years, continued to subscribe to the old colonial way of looking at Indian history. This shows that the major fault-line of the socio-politics of Indian archaeology does not lie along the pre- and post-Independence axis; both Sankalia and Misra wrote long after 1947 but both believed in the colonial framework of the Indian past. Their academic backgrounds also are dissimilar. Sankalia was the epitome of an old-fashioned *Guru/ Acharya* whose education was in the field of ancient Indian history (Ph.D thesis on the historical geography of Gujarat) whereas Misra styles himself different from such historians. In his review of Indian Stone Age in 1989 he writes that "*unfortunately* (italics added), for historical reasons, the pioneering archaeologists were trained in history and their approach was essentially culture-historical rather than anthropological and ecological" (Misra 1989). As far as the history of prehistoric India is concerned, these two Indian scholars of dissimilar academic backgrounds had no hesitation to view it as a continuous process of colonization. It is not even necessary here to refer to Sankalia's devoutness as a Hindu or Misra's importance in the archaeological establishment of India for many years in the 1980s and 1990s. Whichever way we look at it, they looked at prehistoric India only from one long-term perspective, a perspective that was fashioned during the long period of India's colonial rule.

The point we are driving at is that there is no single fault-line of the sociopolitics of Indian archaeology. The fault-lines lie along the different approaches to the past and possibly along different group and class orientations.

If one has to point out a single fault-line, that lies between those practitioners of the subject who want to understand the course of Indian history in its own terms and those who still retain a firm faith in what was the most important colonial paradigm of the historical study of India. One should never underestimate the strength of the colonial paradigm. I have cited the opinion of two Indian pre-historians, both with solid national and international reputations and both far from the 'left' stream of the Indian politics. If one has to cite the similar opinion of a foreign scholar, and that too in a field as innocuous as ancient art-history, one may cite the opinion of Elizabeth Rosen Stone who is known as the author of a volume on the Buddhist art of Nagarjunakonda. In an art-history course in the University of Pennsylvania, entitled "The impact of ancient Near Eastern and Classical art upon the art of India", Elizabeth Rosen Stone wrote the following in the course syllabus section (it was put up on the university website, dated 1997):

> While contacts with the West produced an obvious visual impact on the art of Gandhara, the impact of the Western world can be seen, in a more subtle way, throughout the entire development of Indian art through the 5th century AD.

The point is that this is not an isolated opinion. In a way it is very reminiscent of Vincent Smith's view of Indian art history (Smith 1889) and in the modern period one especially remembers such attempts as to trace the medallion on the forehead of Didarganj Yakshini to a Roman inspiration (Schlumberger 1988; for counter comments and firm support for its Mauryan date, Khandalavala 1988) or the quest to place the famous *Sramana* figure of the Indus civilization in the context of the art examples from Bactria and elsewhere in western Asia (Winckelmann 1994). The 'politics' of the way certain ancient Indian art objects have been viewed has been made explicit in Tapati Guha-Thakurta's analysis of the controversy around the Didarganj Yakshini. The debate is about its date. To many of us, it should be placed in the third century BC and considered a major item of what we call Mauryan art.

> The theme of 'indigeneity' (soon to be inflated into the theme of 'Indianness') became the core issue. Both the signs of the 'primitive' and the 'refined' in the modelling of the *Yakshi* served as compelling metaphors for presenting an ancient home-grown history for Indian sculpture. While her 'primitive' qualities became indicative of an existing indigenous sculptural practice, the 'surprising maturity' of such an early piece would also be read as 'proof' of a prior pre-Mauryan tradition of stone-sculpting in India – stretching back beyond the first surviving examples from the Asokan era. A moot point, here, was to dismantle the long-standing European interpretation of Indian art history, which invariably explained both the origins and the grandeur of the earliest stone architecture and sculpture in India in terms of Achaemenid and Hellenic influences. The dual marks of the 'indigenous/'Mauryan' in our *Yakshi* would become the surest signs of an autonomous national history (Guha-Thakurta 2002: 9-10).

What lends this and many other controversies like this their significance is that this battle between the old colonial approach and the nationalist approach of looking at the archaeological objects of India should be fought out even now on various levels, cutting across national boundaries in the sense that a significant number of Indians still subscribe to the colonial approach. This is a sure proof of the extent to which the colonial frame dominates Indian historical education even today. This also illustrates how Indians of certain types shy away from any interpretation of the ancient Indian past which to them carries an aura of commitment to knowing the history of the country in its own terms. On the other hand, when scholars like Elizabeth Stone carry the tradition of Vincent Smith, that is a clear throwback to the times when ancient Indian history was viewed primarily as a set of migrations and foreign influences. The persistence of this attitude among many Euro-American scholars only illustrates the position of India in the global power-structure, especially in relation to Euro-America.

That the extent to which the idea of migrations has been accepted or denied in the context of the various European national traditions of archaeology was once discussed by H. Harke (1998). First, he contrasts the modern British and German scholarly attitudes to migrationism. Regarding the British situation, he cites the opinion of a colleague of mine, according to whom the British archaeologists were more inclined "to think in terms of an unbroken sequence of occupation and exploitation of the land, rather than the disruption of invasion, simply because it is so long since England was invaded" (Catherine Hills cited by Harke 1998: 20). In Germany the nation-state is thought to be the homeland of a single ethnic group which is defined not by territory but by language and origin. Thus, the German scholars do not find it difficult to imagine the movements of large and homogeneous population groups and the transfer of their ethnic identity from one area to another. The not-so-covert scholarly assumption is that "cultural community equals biological community". Perhaps more germane to the Indian context is Harke's allusion to migrationaism under the Apartheid era in South Africa where the cultural potential of the natives was minimised, the importance having been given to the hypothetical groups coming from the Mediterranean regions or the Middle East. The ruling Boer minority was seen as a part of this migration continuum: "their own descent from immigrants, an aspect so important to their identity that among the Boers it became enshrined in a form of conquest ideology reiterated in semiritual re-enactments and celebrations of the wagon trains of the first settlers, the Voortrekker" (Harke 1998: 23). The Soviet State denied external contributions to the formation of early

Slav culture and early Slav state-formation but saw no difficulty in imagining peoples' movements out of Central Asia.

Thus there are modern political questions in the real or imaginary past movements of people, and the current archaeological interest in both population movements and ethnicity may have a lot to do, according to Harke, with the problem of immigration and asylum-seekers in many countries of Europe.

One would, however, do well to consider that the issues of migration and ethnicity are interrelated and not mere politically inspired innocuous historical ideas. They depict a world-view of history in which the mix of biology, material culture and language appears to be the most important mix behind historical changes. This is plainly a racist view of history, and even an elementary review of this concept will show that the infallibility of this concept dominated the study of history from the eighteenth century to the middle of the twentieth, i.e., the basic period of Western dominance. Most of the ethnic problems of the modern world are rooted in this concept of difference between different human groups. If migrationism and belief in ethnicity have come back to haunt the archaeological literature today, that can only mean that in the modern uni-polar world the concept of superior people bringing about change does not seem as remote as it did in the post-war liberation era and the phase of Civil Rights movement. It also means that, despite the large-scale introduction of science in archaeological research and the archaeologists' professed worship at the altar of 'theory', the archaeological mind has not really been able to break out of the race mould which controlled it for so long.

For the Third World archaeologists in the modern world, migrationism and ethnicity are not innocuous concepts. Many people die in these countries because of the conflicts arising from different kinds of perceived ethnicity and imagined historical trajectories based on population movements. In recent years one of its deadly examples is the genocide in Rwanda whereabout one million Tutsis and moderate Hutus were the victims of racial killings in a reasonably short period in 1994. In the scholarly literature dealing with the history of population in Rwanda, the Tutsis were assigned a more favourable Hamite origin whereas the Hutus were considered inferior Bantu. The Wikipedia article on the Rwanda genocide makes it clear that during the colonial rule the Tutsis were the dominant group and encouraged racial speculations that justified their rule, but that position changed once the Hutus came to power. Now the Tutsis were seen as foreign invaders.

Even as ideas, there never was a rational structure behind such divisions of people; the idea of a relationship between 'race', language and culture was based only on a series of suppositions which suited the ruling philosophy of the day. That it should still figure in the Euro-American archaeological literature which, since the 1960s at least, is supposed to be aeons away from the 'culture history' of the prehistoric era of the subject is seriously problematic. Why should we keep on believing in academic ideas, in the name of which people have been dominated and killed and are still being killed? I have no answer to this question.

In south Asia itself, the assumed difference between the Sinhalese and the Tamilians – an assumption which has eventually led to deadly conflict in the island – is that the Sinhalese are Aryans and the Tamilians Dravidians. Their history in the island is supposed to be different. In India, in addition to the postulate of Aryan-Dravidian difference, which is a major factor to reckon with in the case of the study of south Indian history, there are many other perceived 'ethnic' differences and the history of all of them is supposedly based on different population and language histories. Before Independence, Indian nationalist scholars tried to overcome these differences by harping on the theme of 'unity in diversity' and by trying to underline the contribution of each group to the composite picture of Indian culture. They accepted the equation of race, language and culture. It would be sacrilegious to continue to believe in this equation in the modern context for no other reason that neither language nor culture is related to any biological grouping. Further, a different view of the past based on the sequence of occupation of, and adaptation to, land has to be built up.

Another aspect of the First World literature on the sociopolitics of archaeology calls for some emphasis. The emphasis has primarily been on the situation in the fringes of the Western world – the Balkans, the Caucasus, the Middle East and Africa and the far reaches of Asia, including south Asia, i.e., generally those areas which lie at the fringe of, and beyond the main Euro-American orbit. This holier-than-thou attitude implicit in this gradually increasing bulk of literature generally shies away from exploring the real roots of the problems regarding the past in these areas. In south Asia, for instance, the more or less constant refrain of this type of literature has been on the theme of religious fundamentalism, as if religious fundamentalism is something unique to south Asia and has not affected other areas of the world and their sense of the past. To be fair to the First World scholars in this matter, their opinion in these matters is well supported and vociferously proclaimed by some of their Third World compatriots, especially those with whom the First World links are prominent and long-standing.

Third World archaeologists have also increasingly to contend with a different type of First World archaeology in their areas. Traditionally, archaeologists have been attached to their own areas of study, absorbing throughout their working life the details of the richness and diversity of the past and approaches toward the past in these areas. The number of such area-specialists in the First World academia is slowly on the decline, and in their place we have, increasingly, 'scientists' who are not committed to knowing the past in depth in any particular area but are interested to try out their 'scientific' ideas in various contexts of the world, especially the Third World where such science-dominated archaeological enterprises are still rare. The voice of the Third World archaeologists in the interpretation of the past of their own areas has not traditionally mattered much in the First World archaeological literature. One has only to look up the reference section of publications on the archaeology of different non-Western regions including the whole of the Middle East to appreciate the truth of my assertion. However, the modern 'global archaeology' dominated by richly funded and multi-disciplinary First World archaeological expeditions is, in the name of scientific analysis of various kinds, virtually relegating the national traditions of archaeology in many parts of the Third World, including India, to the position of a minor, often irrelevant, footnote. There is also an undercurrent of racial arrogance throughout.

The study of the socio-politics of archaeology is as varied as the national situations which give rise to archaeological research. It operates on different planes, has different dimensions, and often cuts across national boundaries (cf. Fowler 1987, Kohl and Fawcett

1995, Diaz-Andreu and Champion 1996, Kohl 1998, Meskell 1998, Diaz-Andreu 2004). The purpose of this volume is to examine how this has operated, and operates in modern India.

NOTES AND REFERENCES

1. If one needs an example, one may cite the debate regarding the course of the Sarasvati which finds recurrent mention in the Indian literary tradition including the Rigveda. The existence of a major extinct drainage line from the Indian Siwaliks to the area of the Rann of Kutch, which passed through the Bahawalpur tract of Pakistan and lost the naked visibility of its course in the desert sands of the same area, has been known and written about since the 1880s when R.D. Oldham wrote an article entitled "On probable changes in the geography of the Punjab and its rivers: an historico-geographical study (with a map and a plate)" in *Journal of the Asiatic Society of Bengal* 55(1886): 322-343. This was followed by C.F. Oldham's article in 1893, "The Sarasvati and the lost river of the Indian desert" in *Journal of the Royal Asiatic Society of Great Britain and Ireland* 25: 49-76. That this drainage line represented the Sarasvati river system has also been placed beyond reasonable doubt, and in recent years a separate website has been set up for his related researches on this river by S. Kalyanaraman. One may note that the term *Sarsuti* is still applied to a part of this river system in Haryana. As D.P. Agrawal (1992: 237) puts it, "it is now generally agreed that the present channels of Ghaggar and Hakra systems in fact do represent the old Sarasvati". There is really no historical and archaeological logic to place this river in the Helmand basin of southeast Afghanistan, as some earlier Rigvedic scholars tried to do. Research on this vast and extinct drainage system is a natural field of geographical, geological and archaeological interest, and Gupta 2000-2001 summarizes some of the current assumptions in this regard.

   In 2003 the then Minister of Tourism and Culture of the Government of India, Shri Jagmohan, announced a Sarasvati Heritage Project under which several archaeological sites along its postulated course would be excavated and the Indian portion of this course would be developed as a hub of tourism with a number of "Circles". One is aware that the sites of Adi Badri, Bhirrana and Juni Karan (the first two in Haryana and the third one in Kutch) have been excavated by the Archaeological Survey of India under this project.

   One would think that the geographical, archaeological and geological interest in the extinct course of a major river of the ancient literary tradition of the country would not cause any eyebrow to be raised anywhere, but it is not the case in modern India.

It is possible that the archaeological component of the project was misconceived. For instance, J.P. Joshi, a noted archaeologist of the Indus civilization, was, according to a newspaper report ("Saraswati project may be buried", *The Times of India*, 1 July, 2004), "at a complete loss with the Project's objectives and claims". He is also said to have questioned the postulated connection between Dholavira and Juni Karan in Kutch and the river Sarasvati. I entirely support this questioning. However, the whole thing has been interpreted politically by the mediaeval historian Irfan Habib. His comment on the project has been cited by another news report in *The Times of India* ("Jagmohan sets about bringing Saraswati alive", *Times News Network*, June 15, 2002):

> Habib, who has written extensively on Saraswati, feels the exercise is a 'waste of money'. The Hindutva historians, he notes, claimed Saraswati flowed from the Himalayas and now they are tracing it in the foothills of the Shivaliks. 'This is an attempt by the RSS to make Harappan civilization synonymous with Saraswati culture. It has anti-Dravidian intentions'.

With the electoral defeat of the BJP-dominated NDA government in Delhi and the induction of the UPA government which is dominated by the Congress and supported by the Left, the Sarasvati project has fallen into dark days and possibly been wholly abandoned. Habib's comments cited above represent the attitude of the new government, although one does not know how a general interest in the history and archaeology of the Sarasvati has to be related to the Rashtriya Swangsevak Sangha (RSS) or how on earth is this supposed to be "anti-Dravidian" in intentions. More correctly, this project was possibly devised by certain ambitious officers of the Archaeological Survey of India who on the eve of their retirement persuaded the concerned Minister, i.e., Sri Jagmohan to accept the idea of this project which would ensure that they retained their importance/job even after their retirement. *The Times News Network* report of 1 July 2004 seems to hint at this:

> A pet project of the then culture minister Jagmohan, officials now indicate that it would be certainly axed. Yet, those involved with the Rs 4.98 crore project feel if this was done, it would be grossly unfair and a setback to archaeology and academics. 'The Saraswati Heritage Project' was not part of any saffronisation programme', clarifies R.S. Bisht, project director and former joint DG of ASI.

This project was also one of the issues of enquiry by a Parliamentary committee (*Report on Functioning of the Archaeological Survey of India Presented to the Rajya Sabha on 25.11.2005* (*Laid on the Table of the Lok Sabha on 25.11.2005*) under the chairmanship of Sri Nilotpal Basu, a Communist Party of India (Marxist) M.P. The following is the relevant portion of the report (the original paragraph numbers have been left intact):

Sarasvati Project

25. The Ancient Monuments and Archaeological Sites and Remains Act, 1958, govern excavations in India. The Director General of the Archaeological Survey of India grants licenses to various excavation agencies, both government and autonomous, for conducting excavations on the recommendations of the standing Committee of the Central Advisory Board of Archaeology (CABA). The criteria for selecting a site for excavation are as under: bridging of missing gap(s) in the cultural sequence of Indian archaeology,
    throwing more light on lesser known cultures.
    Salvage archaeology in the event of a site being submerged by a dam or being destroyed or damaged due to absolutely necessary development works, natural calamities.
26. The Committee desired to know the details relating to the Sarasvati Heritage Project. In response the Committee was apprised by the Ministry of Culture that the Sarasvati project aimed at conducting a multidisciplinary study of River Sarasvati and its basin stretching in India from the Sivaliks to the Arbian Sea, falling in the Indian states of Haryana, Rajasthan and Gujarat and formulating and implementing integrated development programmes in the area by creating 15 hub sites as centres of culture, tourism and good civic life. For providing a proper orientation as well as implementation of the Project, the Government of India through its gazette notification S.O. 1329 (E), dated 18 December 2002, New Delhi, constituted a 13 member committee, namely, the Advisory Committee, for the Multidisciplinary Study of River Sarasvati (ACMS), under the chairmanship of the then Minister of Tourism and Culture.
27. During the oral evidence of the representatives of Ministry of Cultural and Archaeological Survey of India held on the 27 December 2004 the Committee enquired about the origin of the Sarasvati Heritage Project. In response, the Director General, Archaeological Survey of India informed the Committee that "the same report was prepared in September 2003 on the basis of the recommendations of a Committee, which was formed in December

2002, with the Tourism Minister as the Chairman besides eight other Members who were experts in various fields and one Joint Director of Archaeological Survey of India as the Member-Secretary or Convenor of the Committee." The Committee then desired to know about the historical and the scientific basis on which the report was prepared. In response, the Ministry informed the Committee that there was a report of the Remote Sensing Agency in this regard which suggested that there was a channel. But the name Sarasvati was not indicated.

28. Not satisfied with the reply furnished by the representatives of Ministry of Culture and ASI, the Committee further enquired from the Ministry of Culture as to whether the Sarasvati Heritage Project was taken up by the ASI under the Chairmanship of the then Minister of Tourism and Culture and whether there was any similar precedent in this regard. The Committee also desired to know whether the Ministry had framed any guidelines in this regard. In response, in a written reply the Ministry of Culture informed the Committee that the project report for the Sarasvati Heritage Project was prepared initially in September 2003 at an estimated cost of Rs. 36.02 crores. This outlay was reduced to Rs. 4.98 crores as reflected in the financial concurrence accorded on 1.3.2004. The Committee was also informed that the former Minister for Tourism & Culture was not the Chairman of the project. The Committee was also informed about the objectives of the Sarasvati Heritage Project. It was mentioned that the Sarasvati Heritage Project was developed as a multi-disciplinary project with the following objectives:

to define the River Sarasvati and its tributaries in the basin by adopting multidisciplinary approach;

to identify special items of geotechnical studies;

to promote multidisciplinary archaeological research by way of exploration, excavation and specialized studies such as ceramic, metallurgical, mineralogical, botanical, zoological, geotechnical, petrological, sedimentological;

to carry out structural and chemical conservation of sites, monuments and excavated structures as well as moveable objects;

to accomplish environmental upgradation of the sites;

realize all these objectives in all integrated, concerted and planned manner under a special drive during a period of three years, to begin with.

29. However, in the same reply the Ministry also stated that prior to the preparation of the project report, the Government had constituted an Advisory Committee on 18.12.2002 with Minister for Tourism and Culture as Chairman and other expert members drawn from outside the Archaeological Survey of India. The Ministry further added that they have not framed any special guidelines for implementation of this project.
30. The Committee enquired from the Ministry of Culture about the procedure followed by the Archaeological Survey of India while selecting a site for excavation and whether they consulted any experts and eminent academicians in the country before finalizing this project. The Ministry replied that the archaeological excavations in the country are approved by the Standing Committee of the Central Advisory Board on Archaeology (CABA) based on the requests for permitting excavations from Universities/Research Organisations. In light of the above replies submitted by Ministry of Culture, the Committee desired to know whether the Sarasvati Heritage Project was recommended by any academic body/university which clubbed this omnibus project under the river Sarasvati Project. The Committee also desired to know whether any proper scientific and technical appraisal for defining Saraswati had been taken or not. In response, the Ministry of Culture categorically informed the Committee that *no academic body or university has recommended the project*. The Committee was also informed that in the past, scientific surveys were conducted in the dry bed of River Ghaggar, identified as River Sarasvati by some geoscientists. There were also remote sensing studies which have established palaeochannels, and the results of such studies have been published in journals like *Journal of Arid Environments, Journal of Geological Society of India, Man and Environment, South Asian Archaeology, Proceedings of the Indian Academy of Science (Earth and Planetary Sciences)*, etc.
31. The Committee further enquired that whether any scientific or technical study had led to the project or certain mythological sources had been used to determine its name. The Committee also enquired as to how a scientific department like Archaeological Survey of India proceeded in this matter, and from where did they get the name of the river Sarasvati. To these queries, the Ministry replied that explorations and excavations in parts of Haryana and Rajasthan on the dry bed of River Ghaggar and River Chautang (River Drisadvati) have brought to light several settlements ranging from the early Harappan times to the modern ones. Besides, surveys carried out by various universities and research institutions like Kurukshetra University, Deccan College, etc. also brought to

light a large number of sites. There were also independent studies by scientists who had made use of the aerial photographs and satellite imageries to delineate the palaeo-drainage course of a river. These studies were published in journals like *Man and Environment*, *Geological Society of India Memoirs*, etc. These scientific and archaeological studies had led to the formulation of the project and naming it as Sarasvati Heritage Project.

32. After going through the replies furnished by the Ministry of Culture, the Committee is of the firm view that Sarasvati Heritage Project did not conform to the criterion fixed for excavation of archaeological sites since no academic body or university had recommended the project. The Committee also notes that there is an element of contradiction in the replies submitted to the Committee by the Department of Culture. On the one hand, the Ministry of Culture has stated that the former Minister of Tourism and Culture was not the Chairman of the Sarasvati Heritage Project, while, on the other hand, the Ministry has stated that prior to the preparation of the project report, the Government had constituted an Advisory Committee with the then Minister of Tourism and Culture as Chairman and that this Committee had recommended the Saraswati Heritage Project. The Committee further notes that the Ministry is not clear as to which research agency/scientific survey actually pointed out that the dry beds of River Ghaggar and River Chautang (River Drisadvati) are the bed of River Sarasvati. The Committee understands that existence of River Sarasvati is purely a mythological one and a scientific institution like Archaeological Survey of India has not correctly proceeded in the matter. The Committee regrets to note that a major project to the tune of Rs. 36.02 crores was prepared which was, however, subsequently reduced to Rs. 4.98 crores just to excavate a mythological river whereas, several other monuments/heritage sites of national importance are languishing in neglect due to acute shortage of funds. The Committee recommends that Archaeological Survey of India should strictly adhere to the criterion fixed for selection of excavation of sites. Further, decisions for excavations should be made on the basis of proper scientific and technical appraisal and no extraneous factors should go into the decision making. The Committee also recommends that before selecting a site for excavation, the Archaeological Survey of India should very carefully examine the potential of the site so that funds earmarked for the same do not go waste. The Committee would like to advise the Archaeological Survey of India that it should prevent itself from taking up exercises without a scientific basis which have all potentiality for subjective interpretation of historical facts, thereby leading to controversies.

What is singularly unfortunate about this report is that here the river Sarasvati has been considered a purely mythological river.

2. This has been the subject of a vast amount of polemical literature in recent years, beginning with S.G. Talageri's *Aryan Invasion and Indian Nationalism* (Talageri 1993) and Bhagwan Singh's *The Vedic Harappans* in 1995 (Singh 1995). This and a few other publications which came in its wake (cf. Elst 1999, Talageri 2000) have been critical of the AIT, as we know it. The 'Indology site' authored by Koenraad Elst on the web contains a separate section called 'Aryan Invasion Debate' which in turn has a number of sub-sections including one on its politics. I find nothing academically inaccurate in the following summation of this politics by Elst:

> The political instrumentalization of theories about Indo-European origins has yielded coalitions of strange bedfellows. On the side of the hypothesis of an Aryan invasion of India, we find old colonial apologists and race theorists and their marginalized successors in the contemporary West along with a broad alliance of anti-Hindu forces in India, most articulate among them the Christian missionaries and the Marxists who have dominated India's intellectual sector for the past several decades. This dominant school of thought has also carried along some prominent early votaries of Hindu nationalism. On the side of the non-invasionist or Aryan-indigenist hypothesis, we find long-dead European Romantics and a few contemporary Western India lovers, along with an anti-colonialist school of thought in India, mainly consisting of contemporary Hindu nationalists. Obviously, among the subscribers to either view we also find scholars without any political axe to grind.

A few other relevant books which tread a different line of thought include Bryant 2001, Trautmann 1997, Bryant and Patton eds. 2005 and Trautmann ed. 2005. The two edited volumes cited here make a great show of highlighting the 'debate' from various quarters, language and archaeology among them. Bryant 2001 is written from the point of view of a person to whom the evidence of 'comparative philology' needs serious consideration. My comments on Trautmann 1997 are incorporated in my article "Further notes on colonial Indology" in C.Margabandhu, A.K. Sharma, R.S. Bisht eds. *Puratana (in Honour of Shri Jagat Pati Joshi)* Vol. 2, pp. 382-390, and for Trautmann ed. 2005 the following comments were made by me in a still unpublished review.

"'The problem with this edited volume on the Aryan idea in Indian history and archaeology is that it does not raise a single inconvenient question about this idea. Personally, I find its banal and holier-than-thou attitude unacceptable. Among other things, millions have died because of the naked racism which lies behind this premise. Nazi Germany is known to have carried it to its logical extreme, but the premise as such was universally accepted well beyond the Nazi world. The idea has sent down deep fissures among the Indian people; one has only to look at the different *Dalit* websites to understand the extent of alienation suffered by a vast mass of Indians because of the socio-political implications of the idea of Aryan expansion in India and its postulated superior Vedic culture. Innumerable books have been written since the late nineteenth century expounding a starkly racist model of Indian history where the history of the Indian civilization has been viewed essentially as the history of Aryan civilization. Taking clues from their Western mentors, the Indian Indologists delighted to wallow in the mire of race-language-culture correlation and accepted the classification of Indian people into neat racial and linguistic categories, trying to assess their contributions to the formation of the present-day Indian culture. In the present reviewer's alma mater Calcutta University it was once customary (it still possibly is) to explain virtually any element of Bengali folk culture as being the contribution of one or other of the linguistic and racial groups, without pausing for a moment to consider how the premise fitted chronologically in the historical scheme of the growth of Indian cultures in Bengal or elsewhere.

Let us look a bit closely at the 'science' behind these ideas. To William Jones, with whom the linguistic origin of the idea is associated, the problem was to relate Indian history to the framework of pre-Evolutionary idea of Universal History where all human groups, because of their descent from the progeny of Noah, had to be related. Jones' emphasis on the similarities between Sanskrit, Greek and Latin is well-known but not so well-known is the fact that in the same sentence he also speaks of Sanskrit's similarities with Peruvian and Japanese! Historical linguistics or comparative philology is a product of the pre-Evolutionary thought. It is interesting that both Jones and Ellis whom the editor approvingly cites, belong to this phase. Similarly, the concept of race also goes back to the late eighteenth century. What is interesting is that the basic ideas of both comparative philology and race retained their structures virtually unchanged till the modern period. As far as the concept of race is concerned, that received a setback after the Nazi excesses and the Civil Rights movement but seems to have entered again through the backdoor in the name of genetics and DNA studies. Such modern studies seem to share an avowed purpose of examining the validity of the nineteenth century racial and language premises in the light of highly sophisticated laboratory data. For instance, in the name of DNA studies, people assert that the high caste Indians are close to Europeans and those born in the low castes lean more toward the Asians in their make-up! Here is the exact sentence in a multi-authored article led by somebody of the Department of Paediatrics of the University of Utah in *Genome Research*, June 2001 issue:

> Analysis of these data demonstrated that the upper castes have a higher affinity to Europeans than Asians, and the upper castes are significantly more similar to Europeans than are the lower castes.

The throw-back to the idea of Indian upper castes being Aryan descendants is clear enough.

Whatever may be the merits of 'historical linguistics', its premises cannot be verified in contexts where there is no writing or where the writing is undeciphered. Of what value is the great debate about the language or languages spoken by the people of the Indus civilization – the Indo-European or Dravidian? The Indus script has not yet been deciphered, and in this matter there is no difference between the attempts of home-bred monks like Swami Sankarananda and those of people like the Finnish Sanskrit professor Asko Parpola. And, why should the Indus civilization be still assessed in terms of its relationship or otherwise with the Vedas? Do the Vedas have any absolute chronology or are its terms amenable to single lines of interpretation? How is it then, that one line of interpretation portrays it as a pastoral society whereas another line of approach depicts it as an urban society? No attempt to pin down the Vedas to any archaeological horizon in the subcontinent has been successful, and there is also no possibility of its ever being successful because of the basic character of the Vedic literature and its uncertain geography and chronology. Again, what is the debate about? The Indian archaeological literature has been full of writings which are all too eager to find the Aryans in some form in the profiles of sites from the northwest to central India, but there are masses of contradictions in them, and nobody except a committed Aryanist would toe those lines of argument. It is, however, curious that attempts to locate Aryans in Indian archaeological record never cease altogether. An American scholar, Gregory Possehl, and his Indian associate Vasant Shinde, have postulated, on the basis of their excavations in southeast Rajasthan, that the area witnessed influence from the direction of north Afghanistan and the area to its north in the protohistoric period. The question is not of academic logic; there would always be some Aryanists inside or outside the archaeological profession."

It is historically important to determine why the controversy has intensified in recent years. I did the following analysis in 2003:

> The historical controversy which is being waged at present in India between the 'progressives' and the 'reactionaries' has shifted from Ayodhya to the Aryans. The issue is related to the speculation about the language/languages spoken by the people of the Indus civilization ... The origin of the Indus civilization on the bank of the Rigvedic Sarasvati may logically lead to the postulate that this particular text was composed in the subcontinental soil and that the people of the Indus civilization possibly spoke a language belonging to the Indo-Aryan family. I have no difficulty with the argument so far, but the 'reactionary' view of things did not stop with this .... India was the Aryan homeland. They fully accept the validity of the Aryan premise but simply reverse the direction of the Aryan movement. The 'progressives' too believe in the existence of a group of people called the Aryans, but according to them, their homeland cannot be in India. In fact, making a claim like this, according to them, is an act of Hindu fundamentalism. Those who consider the Aryan idea to be a plain racist myth – as I do – are not intrigued by the opinion of either groups .... What is relevant in the present context is that quirky academic opinions would not have been a matter of 'progress versus reaction' or 'secularism versus communalism' in modern India unless there was a struggle between the ruling BJP and their leftist opponents to dominate the power structure of Indian historical studies. As the left has currently been dislodged from certain central points in this power-structure, they have been crying out the loudest (Chakrabarti 2003: 204-205).

The Indian scene regarding the Aryans is no doubt torrid where the arguments and counter-arguments of various opponents are not always clear. For a generally correct and less torrid introduction to the major related issues, the following articles in *Wikipedia* may be useful: "Aryan invasion theory (history and controversies"; "Aryan race"; and "Out of India theory".

3. Regardless of the tremendous contribution of archaeology to the study of the ancient Indian past, the dominant perception of ancient India still seems to be rooted in the Vedas. A recent example of the prevalence of this attitude may be seen in the formation (in 1996?) of World Association for Vedic Studies, mainly by expatriate Indians in the United States, a large number of whom are scientists, technologists and medical persons. The purpose of the Society has been stated to be the following:
   (i) Promote Vedic studies in all its forms and in all countries;

(ii) Conduct multidisciplinary activities for the study of Vedic and ancient Indian traditions including its history, philosophy, science, psychology, literature, linguistics, etc.
(iii) Support studies in various Vedic subspecialties such as chronology, ritual, philology, archaeo-astronomy, yoga linguistics, etc.
(iv) Encourage research in all aspects of the Vedic and ancient Indian traditions.
(v) Promote universal, intellectual, and ethical traditions enshrined in Vedas and other works following them.

The formation of such an organization by a group of high-level professionals belonging to various technical subjects has drawn its usual quota of attack from India's establishment historians: cf. Romila Thapar in 'Hindutva and History', *Frontline* 17(20), Sept 30-Oct 13, 2000:

> There is no recognition of the technical training required of historians and archaeologists or of the foundations of social science essential to historical explanation. Engineers, computer experts, journalists-turned-politicians, foreign journalists posing as scholars of Indology, and what have you, assume infallibility, and pronounce on archaeology and history.

Perhaps in return, Romila Thapar as a historian has been examined in a letter by Mr. Vishal Agarwal (an engineer/scientist) protesting against her appoinrment to the Kluge Chair at the Library of Congress, Washington, D.C. (Vishal Agarwal's website). Also by Vishal Agarwal, 'Romila Thapar defends the Aryan invasion theory' in http://www.IndiaCause.com.

Thapar's own views about Aryans are clearly stated in her *Ancient India,* a history textbook for Class VI, National Council of Educational Research and Training, 1 edition in 1987; 10 reprint in 1997). Chapter 3 of this book is entitled *Life in the Vedic Age*, and its subtitle is: *The Aryan Settlements.* Indian history between the decline of the Harappans and 600 BC is discussed under this heading. On p. 37 of this book she writes that during this period a people speaking an Indo-Aryan language (which is the basis of Vedic Sanskrit) emerged in north-western India. "We do not know where they came from: perhaps they came from north-eastern Iran or the region near the Caspian Sea or Central Asia."

Further, on p. 41 of the same book she states that "the horse is not an animal which is native to India and was brought in by the Aryans from Iran and Central Asia ... The Aryans, when they settled in various parts of north India, were hostile to the indigenous people whom they referred to as 'Dasas' and 'Dasyus'."

Thapar wrote her 'Hindutva and history' as a covering article for the article written by her two American associates, M. Witzel and S. Farmer, on the problem of horse in the Indus civilization. On Witzel, the following piece is interesting: "Thus spake Professor Michael Witzel, a Harvard Unversity Case Study in Prejudice" in http://www.vigilonline.com/downloads/Dossier on Witzel.pdf. In any case, for a focus away from the Vedas, attention may be drawn to the attempt made by the Infinity Foundation to study the traditional knowledge systems of India.

4. Rajiv Malhotra, the founder of Infinity Foundation has written extensively on this theme – cf.; "The axis of neo-colonialism" (July 10, 2002, Sulekha.com Blogs); "RISA Lila-1: Wendy's child syndrome" (Sulekha.com Blogs, Sept 6, 2002, RISA being the acronym of Religions in South Asia, a unit within the American Academy of Religions) "Does South Asian studies undermine India" (December 4, 2003 in Rediff.com). These writings will be discussed in a later chapter of the present book.

5. The controversy regarding the Indian history textbooks which are meant for various classes in schools all over India and published by the National Council of Educational Research and Training (NCERT) gained ground first in 1977 after the withdrawal of the Emergency. The attack was spearheaded by S.P. Gupta, a well-known archaeologist but also somebody close to the RSS. As far as I remember, the academic points raised against the concerned publications were really not earth-shattering – in any case, nothing that could not be amicably discussed and taken care of in the future editions. However, Gupta was only making a political point in the post-Emergency period when the people behind these text-books, all belonging to the various shades of the Indian Left beginning with the then Minister of Education, wielded extraordinary academic and political power, virtually throttling any other line of historical thought in the Indian academia. There was absolutely nothing wrong for the NCERT to have framed an all-India history syllabus for schools, but to give the task of writing the concerned textbooks to a few hand-picked persons of the ruling group was not an academic but a political move. This was also a great way to bring financial benefits to the chosen few. The responsibility of writing the textbooks should have rested with the individual publishers and authors. Various books written according to the NCERT-prescribed syllabus would have competed openly in the marketplace, and the best ones would have survived.
The second major battle over these textbooks was fought in the late 1990s and the early years of the new century during the rule

of the National Democratic Alliance dominated by the BJP. The new power group decided to behave in the historical field exactly in the way in which the Left had behaved earlier. A new set of books came into existence, and as they were written by people of possibly lesser academic calibres, they were more inane in comparison with the earlier set of books. It was the turn of the Left now to launch the offensive, which they did rather religiously. One does not know how things stand in 2006, with the Left being back to the helm of historical affairs again. It is however unlikely that the Indian history textbooks for schools will be freed from the rapacity of the historians trying to curry favour with the political masters of the day.

The California Textbook Controversy unfolded, if one knows correctly, only in 2005-2006 and has to do with the way Hinduism and ancient Indian civilization have been depicted in a set of books teaching World cultures and religions in Californian schools. Objections were raised on behalf of some Hindu American citizens/ residents who certainly were within their rights to do so. The opposite group led by the dominant establishment of Indian Studies in the USA and its protègès in the United States and elsewhere categorized all objections raised by the first group as attempts by Hindu fundamentalists to 'saffronize' Californian school books. What one gathers from the material published on the internet that the two core points of the controversy were, first, the Aryan invasion theory, and secondly, the way the Indian caste system and Hinduism were generally depicted in these books. Academically the objections were raised under the apparent coordination by S.G. Bajpai, a noted scholar of Indian origin of ancient Indian history in the U.S. It is also from the internet that one learns that J.M. Kenoyer and M. Tosi were among the scholars who wrote in favour of the Aryan invasion theory and other ideas, against which objections were originally raised. The matter was taken up to the Californian judicial process, and one gathers that the court has ruled in favour of the books being retained in circulation, although with comments on the procedure with which they were accepted in the first place. The California Textbook Controversy proves once again that any attempt to question the generally dominant assumptions regarding Indian history and Hinduism will be vociferously attacked as an act of Hindu fundamentalism. It would have been interesting to have access to the representations made by the two archaeologists Kenoyer and Tosi; one could then try to follow the drift of their archaeological arguments in support of the AIT. The *Wikipedia* has an article under the title "Californian Hindu textbook controversy" with detailed references to the related

websites. The detailed history of the NCERT textbook controversy has been worked out in *Curriculum as Destiny: Forging National Identity in India, Pakistan and Bangladesh*, Ph.D thesis, University of Texas at Austin, August 2003 (the full thesis is available on the web) by Yvette Rosser (2003).
In the context of the controversy regarding textbooks in India, it is interesting to reflect on what P.V. Kane wrote in 1953, almost anticipating what has been happening in India since the 1970s.

> There is possibility of grave harm that might be done to true History by Government action, by political parties, politically-minded citizens and mere theorists. Political propaganda has often made use of History as a medium. Historians may become instruments of politicians and might not afford to summon courage to tell the truth. Recently, I had occasion to read the report of the Zakir Hussain Committee on 'basic national education' (Wardha 1938). That report stated that, as the Indian nation had adopted non-violence as the method for achieving all-round freedom, Indian children would need to be taught the superiority of non-violence over violence (p. 8), that a simple outline of Indian history should be given, that the chief land-marks in the social and cultural life of the people should be stressed and the gradual movement towards greater political and cultural unity be shown and that emphasis should be laid on the ideals of love, truth and justice and on lessons drawn from life showing the superiority of truth and non-violence in all its phases and its concomitant virtues over violence and deceit. I inquired of several booksellers for a copy of a textbook of Indian History in English, Hindusthani or Marathi meant for students in the primary or secondary stages and written on the lines indicated in the Report mentioned above. I could not secure such a copy. Such a textbook would, I am afraid, be guilty of *suppression veri* and *suggestion falsi*. I believe that no honest history can be written about Indian History based on the principles stated in the Report referred to above, particularly for the period from about AD 1200 to AD 1920. It would be better not to teach any History to students for the period before 1947 at all rather than teach a garbled version of History (Kane 1953: 5-6).

6. Among its recent examples one may cite the controversy created by two American archaeobotanists, S. Weber and D. Fuller, regarding the domesticated status of rice in the sixth-fifth millennia BC context at Lohuradeva near Gorakhpur. In a conference organized by the Directorate of Archaeology of Uttar Pradesh Government in the winter of 2006, they cast doubt on this rice being of domesticated variety on the ground of grain size which, they thought, was too small to suggest domestication. They ignored the fact that the evidence was supported by the related profiles

and that rice husk was used in mud plaster of the earliest level. The issue has been discussed in my *The Oxford Companion to Indian Archaeology* (2006), pp. 523-524. What is intriguing is that this opinion was prominently cited in a website associated apparently with M. Witzel and S. Farmer where, if one remembers correctly, doubts were cast even on the radiocarbon dating carried out at the Birbal Sahni Institute of Palaeobotany, Lucknow. The denigration of an Indian laboratory without citing any specific reason and the impromptu denial of the existence of cultivated rice at Lohuradeva throw light on the concerned people's attitude towards India. However, these two archaeobotanists and their associates do not stand alone in raising such issues when faced with early dates for cultural levels in India. I have heard this canard being spread by some other American specialist in Indian archaeology. As far as the credibility of the Lucknow laboratory is concerned, there is absolutely no reason to spread canards about the veracity of its dates. In fact, while setting up the AMS facility at the Institute of Physics in Bhuvaneswar, interlaboratory comparisons of dates were undertaken by the Institute to test its own AMS dates, and for conventional counting method it compared its dates with those derived from the Lucknow laboratory. For the AMS it compared results with the NSF, AMS facility in Arizona (Prasad *et al.* 2006).

7. Further reviews of *Colonial Indology* included those done by Professor C.C. Lamberg-Karlovsky (in *The Review of Archaeology*, Vol. 18, No. 2, 1997), Rosanne Rocher (in *Journal of the American Oriental Society* 118.2 1998) and another American, Daud Ali (in *Journal of the Royal Asiatic Society*, November issue, 1998). One regrets that much of Professor Lamberg-Karlovsky's review is based more on anger than on logic, but let me give some more examples of what characterizes Western archaeological/Indological scholarship vis-à-vis India. I begin with A.C.L. Carlleyle, to whom I give full credit for what he achieved in his archaeological explorations. In his *Report of Tours in the Central Doab and Gorakhpur in 1874-75 and 1876* (1879, pp. 104-105) he wrote the following:

> ... We British Europeans are Aryans, and far more pure and genuine Aryans than the Hindus, and no talk of the Hindus can alter our race, or make us any less or any different from what we are. It is the Hindus who have altered and deteriorated, and not we! The Hindu has become the coffee dregs, while we have remained the cream of the Aryan race. The Hindus are like the monkey, who pretended to treat some men with contempt because they had bare white skins without any fur! The Hindu has become a sooty, dingy-coloured earthen pot, by rubbing against

> black aborigines rather too freely; and he consequently pretends to despise the white porcelain bowl.

Let me cite some more recent examples of more or less the same attitude vis-à-vis Indians/Orientals. J.M. Kenoyer's *Ancient Cities of the Indus Valley Civilization* bears a preface by Richard H. Meadow of Peabody Museum, Harvard University (in other words, a colleague of Professor Lamberg-Karlovsky). After sentimental reference to Kenoyer being raised by a Kuki-speaking ayah and his knowledge of Bengali, Hindi and Urdu, he adds that Kenoyer's portrayal of the Indus civilization is "tempered by Western academic scepticism. Thus we do not see those flights of fancy or long leaps of faith that characterize some literature of the region". Wild flights of fancy are not limited to the subcontinent, in the history and archaeology of which Meadow and Kenoyer specialise, and neither is 'academic scepticism' confined only to the West. It is the prevalence of attitude such as this which makes the writing of *Colonial Indology* a worthwhile effort from the Indian point of view.

In the same vein I would draw attention to J.M. Kenoyer's review of G.L. Possehl's *Indus Age: the Writing System* (in *Journal of Asian Studies*, November 1997 issue): "Possehl's discussion about the direction of writing and the possible family to which the language belonged are uncontroversial (at least to Western scholars ...". Why should Possehl's championing of the Dravdian hypothesis be uncontroversial "at least to Western scholars" as Kenoyer puts it? Are they endowed with some special powers of reasoning?

It may come as a surprise to Professor Lamberg-Karlovsky, but the realization that the Western Oriental scholars had contempt for the natives, which was not good for the interests of the empire, can be traced back to G.N. Curzon, the Viceroy of British India at the beginning of the twentieth century. The context, as Nayanjot Lahiri (in *South Asian Studies*, no. 13, 1997) has demonstrated in her paper on the administrative documents related to John Marshall's appointment as the Director General of the Archaeological Survey of India in 1902, was the question of choice of an orientalist such as Vincent Smith for the job. Lord Curzon did not want an orientalist to be appointed. In fact, he went to the extent of opposing archaeological research in India under the auspices of India Exploration Fund.

"I have not the slightest intention of admitting them to the country ... I do not want a polyglot crew of Germans, French and so on digging about in India, hammering the natives and carrying off our spoil."

I now quote Lahiri's comments on Lord Curzon's attitude (*ibid.*, pp. 133-134).

> Finally, Curzon seems to have attached a low premium on Smith's brand of oriental scholarship in which all noteworthy aspects of India's architectural, pictorial and numismatic arts were seen as being of Western origin. The damage done to the study of archaeology by such scholarship had also been expressed to Curzon by some of the old guard of the Survey such as J.B. Keith ...: "for years the necessities of Indian Archaeology have fallen into the hands of philologists who have made a preserve in pressing home the exploded theories of Professor Max Muller, largely responsible for the exaggerations of the Western civilization".

My contention that Western Indological scenario has always been superior in tone in relation to India and Indians is borne out by the tone of Rosanne Rocher's review, According to Rocher, "the interplay of linguistic and ethnological paradigms in the construction of race in colonial India needs more fine-grained studies". She may be assured that there is nothing remotely fine-grained about racism or even about the reconstruction of race in any context or society. Her sense of dismay with my treatment of the Western opinions on some major issues in the study of ancient Indian history is frankly amusing. These are the opinions with which the Indian academia has lived with so long, and the first sign of criticism exposing the ridiculous chain of reasoning behind these opinions seems to fill her with dismay!

Daud Ali in his review alleges that I have not discussed what he describes as the opinion of "Hindu chauvinists". Hindus are no more or less chauvinists or fundamentalists than any other religious group – Christian, Islamic, Jewish, Buddhist or whatever. Why should Ali pick on Hindu chauvinism and not on many similar kinds of chauvinism and fundamentalism that one finds operating among various religious and/or regional groups in India? The way these groups are ready to interpret Indian history from the point of view of their interests certainly calls for detailed empirical studies. However, that was not within the stated academic scope of my book reviewed by Ali. Again, fundamentalism/chauvinism is hardly an exclusively Indian phenomenon. Why the signs of fundamentalism among an Indian community should form the staple of countless Western analyses of India, some even from Sanskritists?

My silence about R. Inden's book *Imagining India* seems to have upset Ali. I would give a straight answer: books like that are written by a Westerner for fellow-Westerners; as a nationalist Indian I feel no interest in them, just as Bipin Chandra Pal (quoted in *Colonial Indology*) found little of interest or relevance to Indians in the Western Indological writings of his time. Ali further asks: "is the dichotomy of indigenous and colonialist the most important quotient in assessing the social scientific approaches to Indian history". I can give my opinion only about ancient India. For those Indians who are not lackeys of neo-colonial and racist Western Indian studies, the answer is a straight "yes".

2

'Sunrise' in the West: Different Strands of Indian Prehistoric and Proto-historic Studies

One would not normally find any political constraint on something as remote as Palaeolithic and Mesolithic studies, not least in the Indian context which has not yet seen the sense of this Palaeolithic and Mesolithic past being significantly incorporated in the nation's historical image of itself. The question in this area of study relates mainly to the way the Indian pre-historians have viewed the past of their country and introduced elements of parochialism and possibly even regionalism in this branch of study.

I. THE GENERAL BACKGROUND

The study of Indian prehistory began with the geologists of the Geological Survey of India who in the second-half of the nineteenth century were successful in establishing the stratigraphical and typological succession and faunal association of various Stone Age industries in virtually all the major areas of the subcontinent. A climatic dimension was added to these studies only in 1930, and an effort to introduce an absolute chronological scheme in terms of Ice Age and thus glacial successions to the study of the Indian Palaeolithic was made a few years later. The Geological Survey of India had lost its professional interest in prehistory as early as the end of the nineteenth century and had nothing to do with these attempts in the 1930s. However, there were possibly a few Indian trainees in the project on the correlation between Ice Ages and Indian prehistory, and among them, two trainees –

D. Sen of Calcutta and V.D. Krishnaswami of Madras – later showed interest in studying the Palaeolithic sites of their respective areas. They were joined in this area of study by H.D. Sankalia of Pune, whose area of research was Gujarat. Around 1947 the Archaeological Survey of India had a British Director General in the person of Mortimer Wheeler who thought it relevant to include the study of prehistory in the Archaeological Survey of India's official remit. The first prehistorian appointed by the Survey was V.D. Krishnaswami in 1946. In 1949 F.E. Zeuner, a geochronologist of London University came on a brief mission to introduce some representatives of the Archaeological Survey of India and Indian universities to the techniques of Stone Age investigations. The study of prehistory by Indians took off from that point, although the first manifestations of Indian theoretical interest in prehistory are typified by the writings of P. Mitra (nephew of the famous antiquarian Rajendralal Mitra and a teacher of Anthropology department of Calcutta University) and H.C. Dasgupta (a teacher of geology of Presidency College, Calcutta). Mitra's monograph on prehistoric India, published in 1922/1923 under the imprint of Calcutta University is only a matter of historical curiosity but Dasgupta's *Bibliography of Indian Prehistoric Antiquities*, published in 1931 in the *Journal of the Asiatic Society of Bengal* is a very important piece of work, as it is an annotated bibliography and shows that he read up all the published literature till that date – something which cannot possibly be said about the current compilers of long reference lists at the end of their articles/books.

In any case, the Indian prehistorians of the 1950s – V.D. Krishnaswami, D. Sen, N.K. Bose, H.D. Sankalia, K.V. Soundararajan and B.B. Lal, people who published on Indian prehistory in this early stage – were all orthodox archaeologists, and although, on the whole, they produced excellent reports, they never went beyond what the nineteenth century geologists were doing, i.e., establishing the successions of stone tools and their typology.

The point to note is that even now, with exceptions only in the cases of Gujarat, Rajasthan, the Son valley, and the Yamuna valley, the study of the Indian Palaeolithic has not been backed by a rigorous study of its environmental correlates and chronology. What is somewhat curious is that archaeologists and historians who have not had any professional training in geology have begun to comment on the geology of their stone tool-bearing localities. This trend has gone on acquiring strength, and currently, the Indian Palaeolithic studies seem to have lost their focus, being lost in the 'scientific' verbiage of people who were never trained as scientists. The problem does not lie in their basic observations of the stratigraphy and typology; the problem begins when they try to define geological formations and interpret the stratigraphical levels in terms of climate and other issues.

An offshoot of this approach has been the emergence of a group of non-scientist scholars who consider themselves more of a 'scientist' than a mere archaeological field-investigator. The centre of this group appears to be the Deccan College, Pune, with subsidiary centres in places where people trained in this institution have been appointed. The fact that the centre of this group is in Pune is due to some historical reasons. Prehistoric discoveries and the reports on the contexts of these discoveries have not by any means been the sole prerogative of the workers from Pune; a perusal of the successive issues of *Indian Archaeology – A Review* will show that many other institutions, notably the Archaeological Survey of India, had played equally significant roles in the Stone Age discoveries. The area where the Deccan College has had an edge over the other working groups in the field of lithic studies is that, whereas in other places the discoveries were made by people working only on behalf of their organizations and not as parts of organized study-schemes, the Deccan College people in this case were working generally for their Ph.D degrees. "Pre-and Proto-history" of various river valleys and districts formed a popular Ph.D topic in the Deccan College under the guidance of H.D. Sankalia. When these theses were published, either as articles or monographs or as both, they increased the profile of the Deccan College in this field. This series has been followed in recent years by another series on "Quaternary formations" by people mostly without any basic geology background.

Eventually this has led to an apparent group-bias and refusal to acknowledge work outside the group, although this does not seem to apply to the work done in the field by people from outside the country. The group-bias is clearly manifest in the recent issues of *Man and Environment*, bulletin of the Indian Society of Prehistoric and Quaternary Studies, which is based in the Deccan College and published from there. One is not sure if it still retains its pan-India focus and is not run basically as an in-house journal of the

Deccan College. It is also known for a completely uncritical approach to the work of foreign scholars in India. On the other hand, there seems to be a steadfast refusal to acknowledge the work done by fellow Indians, a glaring instance of such a case being the lack of reference to the work of the Geological Survey of India geologists in Himachal Pradesh, Jammu and Ladakh regarding the lower Pleistocene antiquity of stone tools in that region. I have not come across any mention of the significance of B.C. Verma's finds of stone tools in the Pinjore and Tatrot formations of the Siwaliks or of the 2.8 mya date of a tool-bearing locale of Uttar Baini in Jammu in any publication by the Deccan College group. Although there is a long and consistent citation of the British work in the Potwar plateau and the Pabbi hills, the find of stone tools in the Pinjore formation in the Gurha Sahan area of Rawalpindi by M. Salim is ignored. Credit goes to K.A.R. Kennedy for drawing attention to the work of B.C. Verma and J. Sharma in the Siwaliks (Kennedy 2003: 132), claiming early Pleistocene antiquity for stone tools in the Siwaliks. He, however, points out that this stratigraphy was doubted by G.C. Mohapatra and M. Singh according to whom the antiquity of the relevant tools is not earlier than late middle Pleistocene. What is interesting is that Mohapatra and Singh are not professional geologists and in such cases it is the opinion of a Geological Survey of India geologist like Verma which is more trustworthy. Similarly, when S.K. Acharya, a former Director General of the Geological Survey of India, doubted the validity of the supposed association between the Isampur tools and the animal teeth on which the ESR dating of 1.2 mya for the site was obtained, it is invariably useful to rely on such judgements by professional geologists than on the opinion of the excavators of the site who are possibly nothing more than self-proclaimed geologists/geomorphologists.

Some amount of regionalism is also clear in the modern Indian Palaeolithic research. For instance, Shanti Pappu, when faced with criticism of her excavations at the Palaeolithic site of Attirampakkam, tried to justify the foreign participation in her excavations without the approval of the Government of India by writing (in *The Hindu* of 16-11-2004) that this was "a world class excavation" throwing light on *the heritage of Tamil Nadu.* It is indeed unfortunate that the heritage of a particular Indian State should be invoked to highlight the significance of a Palaeolithic site. Similarly, the so-called discovery of Palaeoliths in the Garo hills or the so-called find of Palaeoliths in the Alakananda valley of Uttaranchal must be counted among such claims.

II. THE THEME OF 'SUNRISE IN THE WEST'

Sankalia, the man who began prehistoric studies in the Deccan College, had a clear approach to the study of the Indian prehistoric past. I have already drawn attention to his use of the term 'colonization' in this context and the continued belief in this approach in this institution several years later in the writings of V.N. Misra. Sankalia's point needs a bit of highlighting in detail.

The jacket illustration of his *Prehistory of India* (1977) was prepared by S.K. Kulkarni, the senior staff artist of the Deccan College under his supervision. The painting basically shows a row of human beings, the person in front being a female with a digging stick in one hand and a fistful of grains in the other. The implication is that they in various stages of cultural development were moving towards India.

It tries to highlight the main theme of the book, viz., "the Dawn of Civilization in Undivided India". In the original painting "sunrise" was shown in the west. From here in various ways, the main elements of civilization came to India, according to the present evidence (Sankalia 1977: the inner flap of the jacket on the back).

It is also in this book that Sankalia makes a strong claim for the correlation of the archaeological evidence with that derived from the *Vedas* and the *Puranas*. He also writes that the hunting-gathering way of life was also envisaged and described by the composers of the *Puranas* and the authors of the early and later Jain literature. For example, one of the words for 'earth' in Sanskrit is *Prithvi*, which means that it has been 'made flat' (*pritha*) for cultivation. The king who made the earth flat is called *Prithu*. Thus, what the archaeologists of the 19th-20th centuries have inferred deductively was intuitively visualized by Indian seers some 2000 years ago .... Archaeology, during the last hundred years and more, has shown that the Indian seers had a point (Sankalia 1977: 81).

The point to note that here is a case where possibly the most famous archaeology teacher of India who is not merely a believer in the historical authenticity of the *Vedas* and *Puranas* but also in all the trappings of Hinduism including the astrology of *Bhrigu-samhita* (for this belief, Sankalia 1978), seriously believes academically that the sunrise of Indian civilization took place in the West. Equally intriguingly, when he refers in this context to *the present evidence,* he apparently does not have any doubt or question at all about the quality of this evidence, nor does he spend any time on thinking of the alternative possibilities of looking at it.

It would also be worthwhile to look at how this particular way of looking at Indian prehistory is affecting the study of what is called the 'peopling of India'. This article, available on the web, was originally published in 1997: Gadgil, M., Joshi, N.V., Shambu Prasad, U.V., Manoharan, S. and Suresh Patil 1997. 'Peopling of India', in *The Indian Human Heritage,* Eds. D. Balasubramanian and N. Appaji Rao. Universities Press, Hyderabad, pp. 100-129. Among the authors Gadgil and Joshi belong to Centre for Ecological Sciences of the Institute of Science, Bangalore and Patil and Manoharan represent the Anthropological Survey of India. The abstract of this paper is worth quoting *in toto* because this shows that the unholy mix of biology, language and culture is still viewed as a major way of looking at Indian history, and here everything, of course, is in the name of science.

> We examine the demographic history of India on the basis of a new investigation of mitochondrial DNA base sequences of 101 Indians, in light of the recent synthesis of global genetic history of humans by Cavalli-Sforza and his co-workers. To this population genetic evidence we add fresh insights into linguistic and anthropological pattern based on the People of India project of the Anthropological Survey of India and a review of the pertinent archaeological evidence on waves of diffusion of technological innovations over the subcontinent. The Indian subcontinent has been populated by a series of migrations propelled by significant technological innovations outside India since the first major expansion of non-African Homo sapiens, probably around 65,000 years before present. The likely major migrations include (i) Austric language speakers soon after 65,000 ybp, probably from northeast (ii) Dravidian speakers around 6,000 ybp from mideast with the knowledge of cultivation of crops like wheat and domestication of animals like cattle, sheep, goats (iii) Indo-European speakers in several waves after 4000 ybp with control over horses and iron technology (iv) Sino-

> Tibetan speakers in several waves after 6000 ybp with knowledge of rice cultivation. A notable feature of Indian society is the persistence of thousands of tribe-like endogamous groups in a complex agrarian and now industrial society. In this society populations of dominant groups have continued to grow, while those of subjugated groups may have stagnated most of the time.

They further add that,

> People have of course migrated out of India as well, but these out-migrations have been on a much smaller scale, and mostly over the last three centuries. This is related *to the fact that India has never been the site of any significant technological innovations. A series of important innovations have, over the years, taken place outside of India, innovations which have given an edge to people in control of these innovations, propelling major migrations* (italics added).

In this list of innovations they include the cultivation of wheat, barley, cattle, pig (Middle Eastern origin), rice and buffalo (origin in China and southeast Asia), and iron. It is worth noting that the publication is dated 1997, by which time the idea of all these innovations taking place outside the borders of India could be seriously questioned. Among other things, the archaeological profile of Mehrgarh in Baluchistan was secure by the late 1970s. The idea of an independent beginning of rice cultivation could be claimed on the basis of the Koldihawa evidence by 1980, and as early as 1976 I pointed out in detail the strong probability of India being an independent centre of origin of iron technology. But were people ever interested in looking at the evidence in detail when it came to the question of understanding the process of Indian pre-history? On the basis of what we have quoted about the opinions of a devout Hindu like Sankalia, a leading light of Indian archaeological establishment like V.N. Misra and people from India's 'science' establishments like Gadgil, Joshi, Monoharan and Patil in this matter, nobody seems to have been willing even to examine critically the premise that India has always been peripheral to the world of innovations and development. This is something which the dominant archaeological and 'scientific' establishment in India takes for granted. The question is not whether India had been or had not been a backwater throughout history. *The question is why the Indian academic establishment is not even willing to subject the premise of India's perennial backwaterness to careful scrutiny.*

III. COMMENTS ON CERTAIN GENERAL TRENDS OF PUBLICATIONS IN INDIAN PREHISTORY AND PROTOHISTORY

Also related with this attitude is a general propensity of the Indian archaeological writers to hold on to frankly outmoded concepts, especially if these concepts originated with hegemonic scholars. The space which the assumed dichotomy between the makers of the 'chopper-chopping tools' and those of Acheulian handaxes has occupied – and perhaps still occupies – in Indian Palaeolithic literature is amazing. The hypothesis, first put forward by Hallam Movius in 1948, has had its devotees into the 1990s, although anybody with eyes open would easily have observed the co-occurrence of chopper-chopping and Acheulian elements at many Indian sites including those of the Peninsular regions. In the context of the Siwaliks, G.C. Mohapatra (1985) went to the extent of offering a geographical explanation for this assumed dichotomy: the adaptation of the chopper-chopping lithic tradition to the Himalayan piedmont zone between the MSL heights of 300 m and 700 m, and the suggestion of the Acheulian being a misfit in this 'sub-Himalayan ecosystem'. Although the hypothesis began to be seriously questioned, since the early 1980s (Jayaswal 1982), the way it still crops up in discussions on Indian prehistory shows how the Indian lower Palaeolithic literature has been incapable of breaking out of an orthodox and dated frame of reference.

Irfan Habib's *Prehistoric India* under the series "People's History of India" (Habib 2001) is an important publication in the sense that this is the first expression of a systematic concern in Indian prehistory by an Indian historian. Nowhere, however, in the book is there a discussion on the general significance of prehistoric studies and the importance of this phase from the point of view of later Indian history. There are also statements which cannot be backed by data. For instance, he (Habib 2001: 36) dates the fossil-wood industry of Tripura and Bangladesh between 11000 and 4500 years ago. Where does he get these dates from? This industry still remains undated. The Mesolithic phase is passed over rapidly, and the importance of this phase in Indian cultural scheme is ignored. Regarding what he calls "Neolithic Revolution" at Mehrgarh in Baluchistan, he mentions the advent of pastoral nomads and migrations of people including warfare as the factors behind the beginning of the domestication process in this region. He also makes some unexplainable statements. First, he writes that the teeth of the excavated skeletons of Mehrgarh I and II "showed that these 'first farmers' of India had affinities with the present South and South-East Asian populations rather than the West Asian people". One wonders if the study of teeth would reveal as much. Besides, what are "West Asian people"? Habib is, however, very keen on detecting migrations from Iran in the Mehrgarh profile, and this he finds in Mehrgarh for no other reason except the fact that the settlement of this phase expanded to over 75 hectares. How could such an expansion be possible without large scale migrations from Iran? According to him this was a situation where the new migrants held the earlier people in subjugation but allowed them to continue to live at the site. This, by his logic, could explain "considerable elements of cultural continuity" at Mehrgarh. "The skeletons from human burials of Mehrgarh III show close affinities to the populations of the Iranian plateau, in contrast to the South Asian orientation of the inhabitants of Mehrgarh I and II; and this strongly suggests large scale immigration from the west" (Habib 2001: 56). Regretfully, I have been unable to trace the primary authority on the basis of which Habib makes such statements and am compelled to characterise them as very misleading.

One, of course, understands that Habib, a well-known historian pillar of the Indian Left intellectual establishment, has no problem about explaining Indian history in terms of 'large scale immigration from the west', nor does he have any sympathy for the possibility of early dates of any cultural trait in India. To him, "it is now certain that the early dates from Koldihawa are due to a misreading of the charcoal-bearing strata"(Habib 2001: 62) and that the trail of rice cultivation in India could lead us to China. The only 'indigenousness' that he allows for the Indian Neolithic was in the case of south India. That China and southeast Asia could send the trait of rice cultivation in India was also argued in some detail by I.K. Sarma (1972).

I have previously cited the opinion of Gadgil *et al.* (1997) that none of the major technical innovations ever took place in India.

Interestingly, the historical opinion they cite as their authority is Habib's article, "Pursuing the history of Indian technology: pre-modern modes of transmission of power", in *Social Scientist* (Vol. 20, Nos. 2 and 3, 1992) and in view of the general tenor of Habib's approach to Indian history, one is not surprised that he holds such a view.

The way Indian scholars have viewed the Koldihawa evidence is interesting in its own right. Interestingly, the argument that the Belan valley in the eastern Vindhyas, where Koldihawa is located, was a centre of early rice domestication was propounded by G.R. Sharma of Allahabad University. He had two early dates (and several later dates), falling in the 8th and 5th millennia BC (calibrated) from the site and a continued prehistoric sequence in the area, including wild rice from the Mesolithic site of Chopani-Mando. There was no way his claim could be ignored outright. However, this is exactly what had happened. As late as 1997 M.K. Dhavalikar, although he accepts the idea of independent rice cultivation in India, is unwilling to take this history beyond the early part of the third millennium BC (Dhavalikar 1997: 230).

Dhavalikar, like Sankalia, was a great excavator of the early village settlements of central India and the Deccan, and his discussion on the various related issues is marked by deep insights and close familiarity with the land. However, as far the origin/authorship of the relevant cultures is concerned, his idea is wholly similar to that of Sankalia who tried to explain this origin in terms of West Asiatic parallels of their ceramic designs. That these parallels were not limited to a specific site and even a specific chronology or cultural context did not matter at all. How on earth could one otherwise explain the occurrence of ceramic forms like bowl-on-stands, dish-on-stands and channel-spouted shapes at these sites without referring them to Iran and beyond? He clearly forgets that vessels of these shapes, especially in copper, may still be found in Hindu households. The journey in search of channel-spouts need not involve any wide search for such vessels all over western Asia, especially when not a single identical pottery specimen could be located in that region.

Sankalia and Dhavalikar are not alone in their obsession with the non-Indianness of such shapes. One has only to look up D.P. Agrawal's comparison of the shape of dish-on-stand from his Almorah area material with the pottery of such sites as Hissar and such cultures as the Gandhara Grave culture (Agrawal *et al.* 1995). One also recalls that after he found a few copper arrowheads in Period II of Bagor in Rajasthan, V.N. Misra (1970) undertook an extensive search of West Asiatic sites in search of the possible parallels of these arrowheads. The possibility of their being parts of a metallurgical tradition with origin in the Aravalli itself, i.e., the area of Bagor, did not even enter his mind. When P.C. Dasgupta in the 1960s found a seal with animal motif in the mid to late second millennium BC site of Pandu Rajar Dhibi in West Bengal, his mind ran straight to Crete, from where, he thought, the seal came (Dasgupta 1965). The situation still continues. Sankalia was not hesitant to compare the designs on the Ahar culture beads at Ahar with both geographically and chronologically disparate sites from Turkey to Iran, and similarly, G. Possehl, Vasant Shinde and M. Ameri (2004) do not worry about invoking, for their so-called seals from Gilund, the equally disparate and untenable comparisons with the Bactro-Margiana Culture Complex of central Asia. Interestingly, D. Potts (2005) thinks that these Gilund 'seal' comparisons could also be with the Gulf area, although one cannot be sure how the site of Gilund in southeast Rajasthan would maintain a contact with the Gulf.

Thus, if one takes a broad view, one realizes that the study of Indian prehistory and protohistory in the post-Independence era has always had some major themes running through it. In the field of prehistory it has largely been issues of groupism/ parochialism/regionalism, inability to critically question the set ideas – especially if they were propounded by hegemonic scholarship – and a rather intriguing urge for the non-geologists to be recognized as torch-bearers of the geological approach to the study of prehistory. In the field of protohistory the holy land of origin of every little innovation including such forms as dish/ bowl-on-stands and channel-spouts was west Asia. What is more to the point is that these approaches and ideas cut through a wide swathe of Indian pre-historians and proto-historians, covering people of different political and religious convictions. Devout Hindus and die-hard communists can all be lumped together in this field. "Sun", according to them, has always risen in the West in the context of ancient India.

Is South Asia the only region in the world where archaeologists, historians and even scientists with interest in history have not been hesitant, both in pre-Independence and post-Independence periods, to view it as an area where all the major technical innovations emanated outside it, especially in the West? Scholars who harbour this opinion cover a wide spectrum of political and religious groups. For instance, as far as I am aware, the *Rashtriya Swayam Sevak Sangha* (RSS) had no problem with this approach. Its only concern is to 'prove' that the homeland of the Aryans was India. It is not seriously concerned, at least on the academic level, with developing a systematic India-centred approach to the archaeology and history of India.

What, then, is the reason, and what is the socio-politics behind it? On one level it shows how incredibly poorly India's historical intellect is rooted in the land and how shaky it is to confront major academic issues on its own in this arena. One need not be surprised, because even now historical studies in India are mainly concerned with the history of the country under the British rule, and that too primarily with the help of the British sources. For instance, it has taken the initiative of W. Dalrymple to get explored in a major way the 1857 papers written in Urdu in the National Archives of Delhi. Basic research, based on the primary sources and active field-investigations, in the pre-British phases of Indian history is comparatively much less enthusiastically pursued. The current state of historical studies in India has been recently highlighted by Swapan Dasgupta in his review of *The Last Mughal: the Fall of a Dynasty* in *The Telegraph* (3.11.2006):

> The writing of Indian history was among the foremost casualties – particularly after the establishment. Marxists made empirical research a term of vitriolic abuse. History became the battlefield of grand theories centred on loaded concepts such as feudalism, imperialism and the mode of production.

One is not quite sure how this particular frame of historical studies has developed in India, but in this particular frame the questioning of the existing thought can never be an item of intellectual quest. The basic questioning of the existing framework of the Indian past would need certain academic courage, and unfortunately in the arena of Indian historical studies, such courage would be a rarity. One of the main reasons of this lack of academic courage is almost a complete separation between qualifications and appointments in the history departments of

Indian universities where teachers are recruited mainly on the basis of their caste, region or group/political loyalties. It is not a pleasant and academically invigorating scenario, but it is there. Unless there is a much more awareness of history in the peoples' minds and unless that awareness is reflected in increasing historical investigations of all kinds in the landscape, it is unlikely that we shall witness the cessation of the general intellectual inertia which appears to be quite happy to view the country's past as a kind of appendage to what happened elsewhere, especially in the regions to its west. It is not usually realized that, compared to many other countries of the world, an average educated Indian's consciousness of the country's past is marginal. If this sounds upsetting, I would simply point out the books which are generally available on Indian history. Compared to the innumerable and easily accessible volumes that one can pick up in the Western bookshops on every phase of Western history, the range of Indian history books is very limited indeed.

It is this inertia which never makes us comprehensively assess the implications of the gradually accumulating discoveries in various parts of the land. For instance, although there has been an undeniable chain of evidence for the past several years to justify the premise of the Aravallis as an independent and early centre of both agriculture and metallurgy, one is not sure if the Indian archaeological establishment has yet come to terms with the notion.

The pre-historians and proto-historians whom we have cited could, of course, claim that they were writing things which they did purely in the name of scientific objectivity. Sankalia, in fact, made a great show of Prehistory being a science and giving its practitioners competence to work anywhere, not necessarily in his own area. The point is that they never bothered to look closely beyond the facade of what they thought was objectivity. Basically this also shows almost a total lack of pride on the part of these scholars in the country's material past. On one level, this may be said to be a reflection on the academic stature of the people who came to practice archaeology and history in the universities. On another level, this may also be a reflection on the way the country's post-Independence progress was, and is being visualized by her intelligentsia.

Even if these archaeologists, historians and scientists had shown no evidence of pride in the material achievements of the ancient past of their country, they could have shown at least some serious interest in widening the scope of technical studies on the material remains by incorporating the help of scientists and technologists. Sankalia understood the implications of such studies and successfully established a few small science groups in the Deccan College in the service of archaeology. Wheeler wrote about this need soon after Independence. The Indian left historians no doubt extolled the virtues of 'people's history' or the importance of understanding the material basis of social formations, but had apparently no idea of the basic science-based tools to investigate the material basis of life in ancient societies. Nor were they interested in investigating the scope of the French *Annales* school of historical studies in the Indian context. They were not, of course, concerned with the methods to relate history to the land. One is not really surprised that in the present set-up there is no properly organized national-level institute of archaeological science in the country, and whatever progress has been achieved in this field has been achieved mainly through individual initiatives. What is worse is that many 'science posts' in the archaeology-related university departments have been converted into general archaeological posts. For instance, after the professor of 'environmental archaeology' of Baroda MS University, Baroda – KTM Hegde – retired, it was filled up basically by a historian/ archaeologist. Cases like this are known to have happened in Allahabad and Banaras Hindu universities as well. The Council of Scientific and Industrial Research of the Government of India could easily have set up an institute for archaeological science. The Vice-Chairman of the CSIR holds the rank of a cabinet minister, and at one point the Vice-Chairman was a historian with Marxist leanings. When the idea of setting up such an institute was broached to him (by the present author), he replied that there was no use of thinking along that line as long as he was at the helm of CSIR affairs. The rumour has it that the Secretary of the Radiocarbon Committee of the Tata Institute of Fundamental Research, Mumbai (later at the Physical Research Institute, Ahmedabad) rubbed him in the wrong way, and he had not apparently forgotten this experience even when he was in a position to do a lot for the development of archaeological science in the country. The point is that it is not rational to seek dichotomies between the so-called 'progressives' and the so-called 'reactionaries' among the Indian historians and archaeologists in this context. None of these groups has ever been seriously interested in working out the modalities of working out a true people's history of India. The situation would have been different if they were seriously interested in these approaches and related methods.

3

The Sociopolitics of the Indus Civilization Studies

The sociopolitical issues of the Indus civilization are fought on a number of fronts: the issue of its name, the problem of its origin, the question of its 'Aryan' or 'Dravidian' identity, and its place as the fountainhead of the mainstream Indian culture. Before we turn to them, we must understand the state of Indian archaeology before its discovery, the ideas which came in almost simultaneously with the discovery, and the main stages of research on it since then.

I. THE FRAMEWORK OF THE ANCIENT INDIAN PAST BEFORE THE DISCOVERY

By the winter of 1920 when Dayaram Sahni was sent to Harappa to excavate, the archaeological study of the Indian civilization was complete in several ways. More relevantly to the present context, the entire prehistoric spectrum of the country was more or less understood. There was no confusion about the abundance of its Palaeolithic and Mesolithic remains, and early in the twentieth century Vincent Smith's paper on 'pigmy flints' also ensured that the significance of the Mesolithic stage fell in place. There was no doubt about the abundance of Neolithic remains either and there were ample indications of Neolithic settlements in the south, especially in Bruce Foote's writings. The concept of 'Copper Age' was there too, Hiranand Sastri's articles on the 'Copper Hoards' of the upper Ganga plain being one of its major indicators. To any perceptive archaeologist, the thought of India having a prehistoric civilization before the limits of its documented history could not have been something very remote. The fact that there was a long-known occurrence of seals with unknown writings and art-style at Harappa should have brought this possibility a bit closer. In the case of John Marshall at least, these 'Harappa seals' remained, as we shall see later, a vexing issue (for details, Lahiri 2005; for a general background of the history of Indian archaeology of this phase, Chakrabarti 1988).

More importantly, the basic frame of ancient Indian studies was securely laid down long before 1920 : the historical chronology, the scholarly analysis of the oldest texts, inscriptions and coins, art and architecture, religion and philosophy, 'linguistic and racial history', and whatever other fields of ancient India that one can think of. People also understood the fact that ancient India has had a long history of trade and commerce with different countries in the west, including Egypt in the second millennium BC. The last bit of information occurs in a footnote of the *Gazetteer of the Bombay Presidency*, Volume XIII, Part II (1882), p. 404:

> As early as 1600 BC the Egyptians had many Indian products, agates, haematite, the lotus, indigo, pepper, cardamoms, ginger, cinnamon and Indian muslins.

The idea of Indians trading from west India to Arabia, Africa and Persia from prehistoric times dates, in fact, from long before 1882. In his *Historical Researches into the Politics, Intercourse, and Trade of the Principal Nations of Antiquity, Vol. III. Asiatic Nations, Indians* which was translated from German into English in 1833, A.H.L. Heeren wrote the following:

> Whether the civilization of India reaches back to one thousand years before the Christian era, as is pretty certain, or even to two, which is not improbable, can never be a question altogether devoid of interest (p. 9).

The ancient trade of the Indian ocean was, in fact, the subject of a detailed scholarly book by W. Vincent as early as 1807, *The Commerce and Navigation of the Ancients in the Indian Ocean*. In view of the subsequent impact of the finds of Indus civilization seals in ancient Mesopotamia on the understanding of the roots of ancient Indian trade, it is important to realize that this happened in the context of a trade which was long known for its general antiquity and geographical extent.

Equally significantly, the framework of Indian 'races' and languages was also laid down sometime before the discovery of the Indus civilization. H.H. Risley's scheme, perhaps the most significant scheme of Indian 'races' in retrospect, took its shape towards the end of the nineteenth century and the beginning of the twentieth. Out of Risley's seven Indian racial categories, five bear the appellations of Aryan/Dravidian: Indo-Aryan, Scytho-Dravidian, Aryo-Dravidian, Mongolo-Dravidian, and Dravidian. The Indo-Aryan type was linked to the traditional Aryan colonists of India, while the Dravidian type was deemed the original inhabitants of India, although with the later mingling of other types. In Risley's scheme, the most inferior status was given to the original inhabitants of the land, the Dravidians. This was also the time when India's language history was formulated by G.A. Grierson. The idea of a Dravidian family of language can be traced back to the middle of the nineteenth century when the contrast between the Aryan and non-Aryan India was a major point of linguistic and other interests (for the details, Chakrabarti 1997).

As far as the historical outline of ancient India is concerned, it is doubtful if its basics have undergone any drastic change since the knowledge was synthesised by scholars like Vincent Smith or Edward Rapson. Smith (1924) offered a definitive framework of political history till the immediately pre-Muslim period whereas Rapson (1914), a Cambridge University Sanskritist, did not venture beyond the establishment of the Kushana power. In Rapson's book, the Dravidian and Aryan invasions are a fact.

> Invaders from the west ... have determined the character of the whole continent. In our sketch of the civilization of Ancient India, we shall have to deal especially with two of these invasions – the Dravidian and the Aryan .... Dravidian civilization was predominant in India before the coming of the Aryans (Rapson 1914: 28-29).

The results of the initial excavations at Harappa and Mohenjodaro, and the realization that a new Bronze Age civilization was discovered in India at these sites, had to satisfy a vast body of knowledge regarding the Indian past and racial and linguistic histories which had by now a very long history of research on them and thus a deeply entrenched framework.

II. THE DISCOVERY AND THE EARLY HYPOTHESES OF THE EXCAVATORS

The starting-point is the report on the results of Sahni's excavations at Harappa in 1920-21. This report was published in the Archaeological Survey *Annual Report* for the year 1920-21, which was edited by Marshall and published in 1923. It appears from the reading of the report that it was written by Marshall himself, summarizing Sahni's work at the site. It also appears that, because of the earlier reports of seals from the site, Harappa held a special place in Marshall's mind. According to him, these seals "suggested that at this site we have the remains of a city of very great antiquity and of seemingly quite peculiar culture, as the legends on the Harappa seals are one and totally unlike any other form of script known in India". About 4 feet beneath surface on a slope of the western mound (AB) at the site, Sahni came across some stones bearing Mauryan polish. His trench was excavated only to the depth of 13 feet, but the mound itself, as was noted, was about 60-65 feet high. However, Sahni could infer that the seals, etc. from the site of Harappa were at least pre-Mauryan in date, and as Marshall pointed out, only the topmost portion of the mound was investigated and that 50 feet of depth still remained unexplored. He also noted that the early bricks from the site were in the ratio of 4:2:1: "this convenient proportion of two widths to the length has not yet been met with at any other ancient site in India". In retrospect, I find it intriguing that no notice was taken of the Harappan painted and plain pottery which must have been unearthed considerably in Sahni's trenches. In terms of its shapes, thickness of profile and slip, and painted designs this pottery too was something which was not encountered before at Indian sites, and neither Sahni nor Marshall took note of this feature. When D.R. Bhandarkar and R.D. Banerji separately visited Mohenjodaro as the officers in charge of the Western Circle of the Survey long before Banerji excavated it in 1921-22, they also observed only the Buddhist stupa at the site, completely ignoring the vast amount of pottery which must have been spread all over it. This shows that Indian archaeology of the early twentieth century was not concerned with pottery in detail.

R.D. Banerji's first report on Mohenjodaro was published in the *Annual Report* of 1922-23 (edited by B. Spooner). The interpretative scheme of this report is inexplicable. Arguing that the city stood on the banks of the Indus, he wrote the following:

> The city was built on both banks of the river, but its principal shrines were erected on islands in the middle of it. A cluster of five shrines were built on a group of five islands, lying close together, two of which were excavated during the year under review (Banerji 1922-23: 102).

The famous Mohenjodaro stupa which occupied a central position in a courtyard surrounded by rooms was said to be built on the top of a high (about 40 feet high than the ground level) rectangular tower of burnt bricks. The quadrangle and the stupa were approached through a pillared hall in the northeast corner, from where "a grand staircase ran along the entire eastern facade of the tower and reached the ground level at its southeastern corner". There was evidence to show that the stupa was destroyed by fire. It is possible that there was an earlier structure at the site of the stupa.

Among the finds at this site he lists flint scrapers and cores, beads of various stones, copper and bronze, plenty of pottery, etc. A limited number of seals were found, and he realized that these seals bore "ideograms or pictograms like the seals discovered at Harappa".

One is not sure what Banerji called 'the larger island' but here also he found the ruins of a stupa and its attached monastery. What is surprising is his claim that "these two buildings were also built on the top of a high artificial tower, the retaining walls of which are still 44 feet in height". "Flint scrapers, cores and coins of Vasudeva I were also discovered on this site", and among other finds he mentions numerous fragments of painted pottery and human and animal terracottas. All that he inferred that Mohenjodaro was abandoned long before the Muslim conquest of Sind in AD 711.

What I find inexplicable about this report is his focus on islands and lack of comments on the occurrence of flint scrapers and cores along with Harappa-type seals here. On the other hand, his main concern remained throughout with the stupas and their attached monasteries. His second stupa complex has not been reported by any archaeologist since then.

The definitive picture emerged only in 1924. One of the places where one looks for the preliminary formulation of ideas regarding this discovery is the *Annual Report* for 123-24, which was edited by Marshall, with the relevant portion being written by Marshall himself.

> In the field of exploration, it is natural this year to give the premier place to the remarkable discoveries made by the Department in Sind and the South West Punjab; for it is safe to say that no such epoch-making discoveries have ever fallen to the lot of an Archaeologist in this country. Hitherto India has almost universally been regarded as one of the younger countries of the world. Apart from Palaeolithic and Neolithic implements and such rude primitive remains as the Cyclopaean walls of Rajagriha no monuments of note were known to exist of an earlier date than the third century BC, when Greece had already passed her zenith and when the mighty empires of Mesopotamia and Egypt had been all but forgotten. Now, at a single bound, we have taken back our knowledge of Indian civilization some 3000 years earlier and have established the fact that in the 3rd millennium before Christ and even before that the peoples of the Punjab and Sind were living in well-built cities and were in possession of a relatively mature culture with a high standard of art and craftsmanship and a developed system of pictographic writing (Marshall 1923-24: 47).

The chronology was established on the basis of the already known finds of seals with the same pictographic writing at sites in Mesopotamia. Marshall realized by this time that the civilization his Department had unearthed in both upper and lower Indus valley formed a part of the Bronze Age civilizations which could be traced from here to the Aegean. On the originality of this civilization he had no doubt, even at this early stage of discovery:

> One feature of these remains which seems to me to emerge clearly from the facts before us is that the civilization of which we have now obtained this first glimpse was developed in the Indus Valley itself and was probably as distinctive of that region, as the civilization of the Pharoahs was distinctive of the Nile (*ibid.*, p. 49).

Citing an opinion which says that the Sumerian element was an intrusive element in Mesopotamia, and arguing that "seals, etc. of the Sumerian type" were being found near the surface of widely separated city sites, with multiple strata of occupation below this level, he argued:

> If, therefore, those scholars are right who consider the Sumerians to have been an intrusive element in Mesopotamia, then the possibility is clearly suggested of India proving ultimately to be the cradle of their civilization, which in its turn lay at the root of Babylonian, Assyrian and Western Asiatic culture generally (*ibid.*, p. 50).

He conceded that it was "obviously far too early" to regard this hypothesis as "no more than a reasonable hypothesis", but was astute enough to feel even at this early stage that the civilization discovered in the Indus valley represented "a development reaching back incalculable centuries on Indian soil".

Among the other features of this report one notes a general reference to the possible religious ambience of the civilization. Mention is made of Banerji's discovery of a tank at Mohenjodaro (although Banerji in his report does not mention this himself), which Banerji is said to have interpreted as a *charanamritakunda*, i.e., "a receptacle for the holy water used for the washing of the sacred image". In the 5th stratum from the top at the mound A-B at Harappa a small chamber with a narrow covered drain in its south wall and two low masonry benches on the inside seemed "to point to its having been used as some sort of an image shrine, though it is difficult as yet to say whether idol worship existed in those early times". The clue is unmistakable. Even then there was no mental barrier to seek the reflection of the religion of this civilization in the prevailing rituals of Hinduism.

III. THE PERIOD BETWEEN THE DISCOVERY AND ASSOCIATED REPORTS, AND THE PUBLICATION OF MARSHALL'S MOHENJODARO REPORT IN 1931: R.P. CHANDA

The Archaeological Survey of India published two memoirs during this period, both by one of its own senior officers, R.P. Chanda. The first one, *The Indus Valley in the Vedic Period* was published in 1926, and the second one, *Survival of the Prehistoric Civilization of the Indus Valley*, in 1929. Chanda was then the Superintendent of the Archaeological Section of the Indian Museum in Calcutta, and by that time he was a *Raibahadur*, an honorary title bestowed by the government. In the first memoir Chanda has two major contentions. First, he assumes that "nothing as yet discovered affords any indication that the builders of the prehistoric cities at Harappa and Mohenjodaro were akin to the Rigvedic Aryas", and following this, argues that "the civilization of those builders appears to be of a non-Vedic type". Secondly, his basic point of query was to ascertain if the Rigvedic hymns contained "any evidence to show that the Rigvedic Aryas came in contact with an older civilization in the Indus valley." Under this heading he cites a number of points, beginning with the mention of the *Yadus* and *Turvasas* in the Rigveda where they were supposedly brought by Indra over the sea. On the assumption that this denotes their origin in the southern region, he writes that these two groups of Rigvedic people were "descendants of immigrants from the south" and thus, he thought, it could be inferred that "the region south of the Punjab was recognized as a home of civilization" in the Rigvedic world. He gets around the problem of the meaning of *Samudra* as "sea" by citing an opinion that the Indus, after it was joined by all her tributaries, was, in its lower or southern portion, as vast as the sea or *Samudra*.

Secondly, he draws attention to the occurrence of terms *Pura* and *Pur* and the fact of their being overthrown by Indra. For instance, for Purukutsa, the chief of the Purus, Indra destroyed seven autumnal *Puras* with thunder weapon, slew *Dasas* and gave wealth to Purukutsa. Chanda thinks that these two terms denoted *Nagara* or cities. On the basis of this and a few other examples, he writes,

> The recovery of the ruins of cities at Harappa and Mohenjodaro leaves no room for doubt that the Rigvedic Aryas were familiar with towns and cities of aliens. It is futile to seek any more historical elements in the legends of Divodasa and Purukutsa than perhaps the names of these heroes. But if we eliminate the mythical and fanciful additions there is no reason to doubt the possibility of the nucleus. There existed and the folk memory remembered that there once existed Arya worshippers of Indra who waged wars against civilized aboriginal neighbours living in towns and fighting from within strongholds. Who, then, were these enemies of the Aryas? (Chanda 1926: 4).

In response to this question he identifies the Rigvedic merchant class of Panis as "the aboriginal towns folk with whom the Aryas came into collision in the Indus valley". Arguing that trade was not a part of the life of the Rigvedic priests and warriors, the only two main classes of people in the Rigveda (according to him), he thinks that the conclusion of the Panis being the representatives of an earlier commercial civilization seemed irresistible. They represented "this prehistoric civilization of the Indus valley in its last phase when it came in contact with the invading Arya civilization". In the second millennium BC, which he thought was the date of the Rigveda, there were "successive waves of, invaders of Aryan speech" across the northwest.

> These invaders who in the Rigveda call themselves Arya met in the southern part of the valley a civilized people who lived in cities and castles and mainly depended on commerce for their livelihood. The Arya conquerors who were inferior in material culture either destroyed the cities or allowed them to fall into ruin. Their great god Indra is called Puroha or Purandara, 'sacker of cities'. Like the prehistoric civilization of the Aegean, the prehistoric civilization of the Indus valley also failed to survive the shock of the Aryan invasion (Chanda 1926: 5).

Chanda goes a step further. He rummages among the Later Vedic literature including the Sutra literature to discover that the Gandhara, Punjab and Sind areas came to be considered as inhabited by people of mixed origins by the later Vedic times. The ritual status of the people of these areas was low, and from this he infers that, just as "the Aryas destroyed the great fabric of the prehistoric civilization of the Panis of the Indus valley", later immigrants all but overthrew the Arya culture in turn in the same region. Most interestingly, Chanda notes that along with the people of Panjab and Sind and the northwest, the later Vedic texts also put the people of Bengal and Orissa in this category.

According to Chanda, there were successive waves of Aryan immigrants and the different modes of disposal of the charred bone relics of the dead, of which he cited some examples from the concerned literature including the Brahmana literature – urn burial, earth-burial and cremation – were possibly related to "different strands of culture" According to him, the urn burial could possibly be attributed to "the influence of the burial customs of the copper age people of the lower Indus valley".

A few broad themes emerge from this monograph by Chanda. The Indus civilization was both pre- and non-Vedic. The Rigveda belongs to the second millennium BC and was the product of Arya worshippers who were settled mainly in the upper Indus valley and associated tributaries, i.e., the Punjab of British India and the northwest. He finds a clear reflection of the destruction of the Indus civilization cities and forts in the references to Indra as Purandara or 'destroyer of forts'. He identifies the makers of this civilization with the merchant group of Panis mentioned in the Rigveda. But what comes dominantly across is the fact of multiple waves of Aryan invaders. They all but overrun the earlier fabric of the Arya culture in the Indus valley and the northwest, bringing down the ritual status of the inhabitants of this region in the eyes of the earlier Vedic orthodoxy. Such later immigrants also brought about different modes of disposal of the dead in the broad spectrum of the Vedic literature, and the urn-burial mode was possibly adopted from the surviving elements of the Indus civilization itself.

In a sense, Chanda's exercise in relating the just-discovered Indus civilization to the framework of the Vedic literature and the postulated Aryan migration or invasion of India is very clearly rooted in his earlier publication, *The Indo-Aryan Races* where he argued that a later group of Aryans, finding the midlands already occupied by the earlier Aryan invaders, went round the earlier zone of occupation and settled down in the peripheral regions in the west and the east, thus putting, for instance, the inhabitants of Gujarat and Bengal in the same Aryan category. This is the reason why he repeatedly insists on the idea of successive waves of Aryan immigrants or invaders – he uses both terms – and makes them appear as meaningful ideas in relation to the Indus civilization. The importance of this exercise does not lie in what he actually said or speculated but in the fact that the idea of the Indus civilization being pre- and non-Vedic became from now on a well-established part of the archaeological thought. The idea of the Aryans destroying the cities of the Indus civilization is also firmly rooted in this publication.

At the same time, Chanda also highlights the possible field of interaction between the Aryas and the earlier Indus civilization people. *Panis* like the *Yadus* and *Turbasas* were said to be incorporated in the Arya frame which also derived their practice of urn burials from the remnants of the civilization they brought to an end. So, on one level, he could not go beyond the dominant framework of the Aryan invasion of India and its chronology and related the end of the Indus civilization to the coming of the

Aryans. On the other hand, he was trying to inject an element of co-existence and perhaps even co-operation between them.

It is this strain of interaction and co-existence which gains primary importance in Chanda's second monograph, *Survival of the Prehistoric Civilization of the Indus Valley* in 1929. The question he begins with is what became of the authors of the Indus civilization "when the Aryan immigrants who offered sacrifices to the Devas and cremated their dead occupied the land". Did the contact between Aryan and pre-Aryan cultures result in the birth of "the mixed Hindu civilization"? His first area of enquiry is the so-called conflict between the Aryans and the non-Aryan aborigines (called *Dasas* and *Dasyus*) in the texts. He points out that the demons are also called *Dasas* and *Dasyus* in the Vedas, and there was more of tussle between the gods and demons than between men and men. "Of these rare conflicts between men and men, again, perhaps as many are waged by the Aryas against other Aryas allied to the *Dasas*." This is an important point, completely negating the idea that the conflict with the *Dasas* and *Dasyus* meant conflict with the non-Aryan aborigines. On the basis of a close study of the contexts of the Rigvedic hymns he demonstrates that these terms were then basically abusive words to denote, from the point of view of the Rigvedic priests, godless and riteless men.

> When the Rishis condemn even the *Dasas* and *Dasyus* as 'godless', 'riteless', etc. they do so more as disappointed priests who have not been paid *dakshina* or sacrificial fee than as missionaries of a higher religion. Thus in Rigveda V.7.10 it is prayed, "O Agni, may then Atri overcome the *Dasyus* who do not give; may Isha overcome the men (who do not give) (Chanda 1929: 4).

He goes on to elaborate that the kings and warrior clans frequently fought among themselves in the Rigveda and there was rivalry even between the Rishis or sages for winning royal patrons. Regarding the frequently expressed opinion that the Rigvedic references to the conflict with the *Dasas* and *Dasyus* do not reflect any ongoing conflict with the pre and non-Aryan inhabitants of the Indus valley. On the contrary, by the Rigvedic period the society was clearly settled and free of strife with the earlier inhabitants of the land.

> But the mutual relations of the different sections of the population of the upper Indus valley in the early Rigvedic period as revealed

> in the hymns of the 'family books' of the Rigveda indicate that the racial animus that once divided the immigrant and the indigenous population of the country was then a thing of the long-forgotten past. The descendants, both of the immigrants and the natives, were reconciled and assimilated as inhabitants of a common motherland, and the wars and feuds known to the poets of the Rigveda were wars and feuds that are inevitable among the different states and classes of the population of a regularly settled country that is free from the fear of foreign invasion. The words *Dasa* and *Dasyu* in the Rigveda denote human enemies as well as atmospheric demons. So it is not always possible to determine whether the terms denote human and where non-human beings .... The *Dasa* or *Dasyu* may be taken to denote human being with certainty in those passages only wherein he is found to fight side by side with the Arya against a common foe (Chanda 1929: 8).

Having argued that in the Rigvedic period the people of the Indus civilization lineage and the people who composed the Rigveda were living together in peace, Chanda turned his attention to the demonstration of how certain ideas of the later Brahmanical Society could come down from the Indus civilization. The first example he takes up is that of the priest and the king. The separation of their roles is clear-cut in the Rigveda where the kings did not have any priestly role, as they had in other ancient societies. This role was given over entirely to the Rishis. Chanda infers a situation where the Indus civilization kings came in contact with the Aryan Rishis, found the gods of the Rishis more powerful than their own, and handed over all sacrificial responsibilities to them. This was how the division between the Kshatriyas and the Brahmins came up, according to Chanda's explanation of the beginning of the caste system. He goes on to analyse the rituals of 'human sacrifice' and *anumarana* (where the wife accompanies her husband to death) in the relevant texts to argue that these rituals were disliked by the Brahmanical tradition but found a favourable hearing among the Kshatriyas. The implicit suggestion is that these two ritualistic traditions are rooted in the Indus civilization from where the Kshatriya caste sprang.

Here, Chanda's scheme to explain the interaction between the Aryans and the Indus people is remarkably striking:

> ... on the eve of the Aryan immigration the Indus valley was in possession of a civilized and warlike people. The Aryans, mainly

> represented by the Rishi clans, came to seek their fortune in small numbers more or less as missionaries of the cults of Indra, Varuna, Agni and other gods of nature and settled in peace under the protection of the native rulers who readily appreciated their great merit as sorcerers and employed them to secure the assistance of the Aryan gods against their human and non-human enemies by offering sacrifices with the recitation of hymns. Now, if the hymns of the Rigveda enable us to reconstruct the proto-history of the Indus valley in this way, the relics of an advanced pre-historic civilization unearthed at Harappa on the Ravi and Mohenjo-Daro in Sind warrant us in taking a further step and recognizing in the warrior clans – the Bharatas, Purus, Yadus, Turvasas, Anus, Druhyus and others celebrated in the Rigveda the representatives of the ruling class of the indigenous chalcolithic population (Chanda 1929: 25).

He goes on to write that the proofs of "a link between the Vedic traditions and the relics of the chalcolithic civilization of the Indus valley" would be required before his hypothetical reconstruction could be said to be vindicated. A part of this link can be seen in the way some stone statuettes from Mohenjodaro, especially the famous *Sramana* figure, unequivocally imply a knowledge of what came to be considered in the *Srimadbhagavatgita* as *Dhyana-Yoga* (*Dhyana* = contemplation; *Yoga* = concentration). This has wide ramifications in Indian philosophical and religious literature from the Upanishadic phase onwards, forming a core concept of Brahmanical, Buddhist and Jaina traditions. Chanda further points out that there are references to two types of mendicant figures in the Vedic literature – the *Vratyas* and the *Yatis*. He finds echo of the *Yatis* in the Mohenjodaro stone statuettes.

He also recognizes "the prototype of the images of Buddha and Jina" in the 'priest' figure of Mohenjodaro but argues that this did not occur in isolation: "other elements of Buddhism, or rather the primitive background of Buddhism, are also traceable in the chalcolithic religion of the Indus valley" (Chanda 1929: 34). Among such elements he points out the significance of the *Pipal* tree both in Buddhism and the Indus civilization. The Buddha obtained Enlightenment under a *Pipal* tree or what is called in the Buddhist tradition *Bodhi* tree. The significance of the *Pipal* leaf and tree is well-understood in the context of the Indus civilization. Another element of this kind is "the cult of the free standing pillar crowned by animal figure (animal standard)" (Chanda 1929: 34). The evidence of such pillars is clearly known from the Indus seals and so do they occur in the Maurya and Sunga pillars. As he puts it, "the temptation to connect the Mauryan and Sunga tree and pillar cults with the tree and pillar cults of the Chalcolithic period in the Indus valley is irresistible" (Chanda 1929: 35).

He understands the huge chronological gap between the two phases but writes that "we have to set off against this absence of connecting links for so long a period the fundamental continuity that characterises the Indian culture" (Chanda 1929: 35). He also tries to question the dating of the beginning of the Vedic tradition around 1200/1500 BC. Citing the famous historian of the Sanskrit literature, M. Winternitz, he argues that "the beginning of this development" may have to be dated about 2000 or 2500 BC, and the end of it between 750 and 500 BC.

In retrospect, Chanda's small monographs are more important than we have given them credit for. They mark the first major attempt to view the Indus civilization within the framework of the Indian tradition. He accepts the idea of the coming of the Aryans but sees it more as a process of acculturation than conflict of any kind. By identifying the Yogic tradition of the Indus civilization, he pinpointed the Indus roots of one of the most significant spiritual dimensions of India, and he also realized how both the Buddhist and the Jaina traditions are indebted to this civilization for some of their cardinal ideas. On a more direct level, he attempted direct correlation between this and the Vedic tradition. This part is purely speculative, but Chanda realized that the Indus civilization could be understood only within the overall context of Indian history and culture. One may also note that he was not happy to date the Rigveda around 1200/1500 BC; the third millennium BC was a more likely date of this text for him.

IV. THE FORMULATION OF THE DRAVIDIAN HYPOTHESIS: SUNITI KUMAR CHATTERJI

The Dravidian hypothesis which was formulated on the basis of Robert Caldwell's linguistic studies in the mid-nineteenth century entered the Indus civilization scene almost as soon as it was discovered. Marshall's famous *Illustrated London News* article on the discovery was published in October 1924, and the Calcutta magazine *The Modern Review* carried in its December issue for the same year an article called "Dravidian origins and beginnings of Indian civilization" by a Calcutta linguist, Suniti Kumar Chatterji (Chatterji 1924).

He begins by citing Bishop Caldwell's publication on the comparative grammar of the Dravidian languages in 1856, which argues on the evidence of purely Dravidian words "that the non-Aryan had a culture, and that of a high standard too, independent of the Aryan one". In the next stage he mentions the point of difference between the Vedic religion and the later form of Hinduism. Among other things, he draws a distinction between the Vedic *Soma* sacrifice and the later Hindu "*Puja*, the ordinary Hindu ritual of worship, in which libations of water, flowers, leaves, and fruits of trees, of grain and vegetarian cooked food, incense and perfume are offered to the God who is actually present in his or her symbol or image before the worshippers, and this symbol or image is treated as if it were endowed with reason, and were a living being".

He goes on to add that "*Puja* is unknown to the Aryan world of the Veda" and eventually writes the following:

> That there was in this way a profound influence exerted by the non-Aryans in the evolution of the Hindu culture and ideas is now gradually becoming a matter of general admission and acceptance (Chatterji 1924: 668).

In the next stage his argument is that the bulk of this non-Aryan contribution could come only from the Dravidians: "it is they, more than any other people in India, who have contributed elements in synthesis of Hindu culture on its Aryan basis" (Chatterji 1924: 669).

He then points towards the Iron Age burials of Aditttanallur or Adichchanallur, which, he thinks, went "to the beginning of the Iron Age, which was certainly before 1000 BC". He also suggested that the Adichchanallur burials were not isolated; their "affinities with Crete and Cyprus seem to be greater, in the crouching position of the dead body, in the sarcophagi and in the golden masks and ornaments (head-bands)". Further, "by measurement, Adittanallur skulls have been found to agree with the typical Tamil skull".

Then follows a description of what was excavated at Mohenjodaro and Harappa, which led to the following conclusion:

> The Mohenjodaro and Harappa culture does not seem to be Aryan. The burial customs are distinctly un-Aryan; they show a deep-rooted difference in racial and cultural origins. When the half-pastoral half-agricultural Aryan barbarians were invading and fighting in North Mesopotamia and then later were settling in Eastern Iran, Gandhara and the Panjab, the Mohenjo-Daro and Harappa people were a flourishing community in the fertile valley of the lower Indus. The Aryans came into India, and as we see from the Rig-Veda and other literature, they expanded East into the Ganges valley, and South-east into the Vidarbha country on the eastern side of the desert. It is strange that no Aryan states grew up in Sindh in the Vedic and Brahmana periods, that there was no early expansion of the Aryans southwards along the Indus. The desert kept them back from Rajputana, where only the Rajputs retired rather than submit to the Turk. There seems to have been present some other factors to hold them back from South-Western Panjab and Sindh and to force them to direct their conquering, colonising and state-building energies to the East and the South-east. It is very likely that it was a strong, and well-organized non-Aryan people in the South, such as the Mohenjodaro and Harappa people would seem to have been. And they could have been Dravidians only. The Brahuis are a direct evidence. And Alexander the Great met with a tribe called the *Arabitai* in South Baluchistan. This name recalls the name given by the Telegus to the Tamils, *Arava*. (Chatterji 1924: 678).

As far as arguments go, Chatterji did not have any argument except a firm faith in all that the linguists have inferred about India's language history. That he could find generic similarities between the finds from Adichchanallur, Mohenjodaro-Harappa, west Asia and the Mediterranean speaks a volume for the ideas of cross-cultural comparisons imbibed by him. It is also interesting that he associated the Dravidians or the Dravidian language-speakers only with the Tamils. Otherwise he could not find any similarity between the Greek name of a tribe in Baluchistan and the term used by the Telugus for the Tamils.

Interestingly, the idea of Dravidian authorship of the Indus civilization has been attributed by him to R.D. Banerji. One does not know where Banerji published his views. Considering that Chatterji was attributing this opinion to Banerji as early as

December 1924, he must have given expression to his opinion before that, possibly soon after his excavations at Mohenjodaro. The report on his work at the site in the *Annual Report* of 1922-23 bears no mention of this theory. It is possible that Chatterji discussed the issue personally with Banerji in Calcutta.

V. OBSERVATIONS ON CHANDA AND CHATTERJI

It is indeed remarkable that within the first few years of the announcement of the discovery of the Indus civilization scholars were trying to locate it both within the frame of the Vedas (Chanda) and outside it (Chatterji). Chanda who published later does not even bother to refer to Chatterji's Dravidian hypothesis; he was content to examine the internal evidence of the Vedic tradition and hypothesize about the possibility of its link-up with the civilization. Chatterji's only concern was that it was an expression of non-Aryan contribution to Indian culture, and that the concerned non-Aryan group was a particular section of the Dravidian-speakers, the Tamils. In a way both looked at this civilization from the point of view of Indian tradition or Indian history and culture. In a sense these ideas formed the backdrop to John Marshall's formulations in *Mohenjodaro and the Indus Civilization* in 1931. It may, however, be noted that Chatterji's idea that the burials were unknown in the Vedic tradition and that there was no 'Aryan' state in Sind was pointed out to be wrong by A.C. Das shortly after the publication of Chatterji's article (Das 1925). Chatterji was only a philologist to whom the conclusions of 'comparative philologists' of his day were sacrosanct. The argument that the form of Hindu *Puja* is a 'Dravidian' contribution to Indian culture and religious life is not based on any historical evidence. Chanda shows a far better awareness of both the texts and the results of archaeological discoveries, and although his chain of reasoning is basically subjective, the way he demonstrated the elements of continuity of the Indus tradition in later Hinduism and Buddhism and Jainism was a fundamental contribution to the understanding of the Indus civilization.

VI. JOHN MARSHALL'S "MOHENJODARO AND THE INDUS CIVILIZATION" (1931)

This publication sets seal on the indigenous Indian roots and character of this civilization. The contemporary anthropological opinions on the 'racial composition' of Mohenjodaro and Harappa were summarised, but no conclusion was formed regarding the 'prime author', if any, of this civilization.

> It may be, nay it is more than likely, that this civilization was the offspring, not of any one race in particular, but of several – born, perhaps, rather of the soil itself and of the rivers than of the varied breeds of men which they sustained. For, as far back as its history can be traced, the population of Sind and the Panjab has been a blend of many diverse elements, and there is no reason for assuming that it was other than heterogeneous in the earlier age with which we are now concerned (Marshall 1931: 108-109).

He briefly passes over the Indus people's supposed similarity with the Sumerians and Dravidians. There was no definable 'Sumerian' physical type, and the same is true, as he points out, of the Dravidian type.

> What, in effect, is the supposed similarity of type between these two races – the Sumerian and the Dravidian – which is coming to be an established fact? ... The modern Dravidian stock is officially described as being "of short stature, complexion very dark, approaching black; hair plentiful, with an occasional tendency to curl; eyes dark, head long, nose very broad, sometimes depressed at the root but not so as to make the face appear flat". It would be absurd to assume that this represents the Dravidian type of 5000 years ago. (Marshall 1931: 109).

Regarding the Dravidian-speaking Brahui population he points out that they could have spoken a Dravidian language but "entirely failed to preserve their racial character" which had now become 'Iranian'. The Dravidian type in the south too had been 'largely transformed by the free admixture of aboriginal, i.e., Proto-Australoid blood as well perhaps as of other elements". In fact, the difference between the Dravidians and the Proto-Australoids was somewhat impossible to define. Referring to both the 'invasion' and 'indigenous' theories of the origin of the Dravidian population, he asserts that it would obviously be very rash in the present uncertain state of our knowledge to endeavour to identify as 'Dravidian' either the skulls classed by Colonel Sewell as Proto-Australoid ... or those classed as Mediterranean ...; rather still to identify any of these skulls as 'Sumerian' (Mashall 1931: 110).

The main reason why he found the Indus and Vedic cultures 'unrelated' was that the Vedic culture, as represented by the Rigveda, was partly agricultural, partly pastoral and had not yet emerged out of the village state, whereas the people of Mohenjodaro and Harappa had lived in crowded cities. The comparisons went on like this, and eventually he posed the problem in the following fashion:

> ... we are wholly at a loss to explain how the Indo-Aryans came to relapse from the city to the village state, or how, having once evolved excellent houses of brick, they afterwards contented themselves with inferior structures of bamboo; or how, having once worshipped Siva and the linga and the Mother Goddess, they ceased to do so in the Vedic period, but returned to their worship later; or how, having once occupied Sind, they subsequently lost all memory of that country and of the Lower Indus (Marshall 1931: 112).

What emerges very clearly from the preceding survey is that by 1931 when Marshall's Mohenjodaro report was published, the question of the affiliation of the Indus civilization in terms of two main groups of Indian languages – the Dravidian and the Indo-Aryan – was discussed and the discussion pattern had already taken a shape which, as we shall see later, has continued to this day. It is interesting that nobody raised the issue of its affiliation with the third major Indian language group – the Kol or the Mundari. S.K. Chatterji seems to have been aware of the issue but contented himself by writing that the Dravidians were culturally much superior to the Kols, implying that there was no possibility of the Indus civilization ever being affiliated to the Kol/Mundari language-speakers.

VII. THE BASIC HISTORY OF THE IDEA OF HARAPPA-VEDIC RELATIONSHIP: B.N. DATTA TO P.V. KANE AND OTHERS

In 1936-37 B.N. Datta [A.M. (Brown) and Ph.D (Hamburg)] undertook a detailed analysis of 'Vedic funeral customs and Indus valley culture' in *Man and India*. He was a member of *Anushilan Samiti*, a secret revolutionary organization of Bengal in the first quarter of the twentieth century. It was established in 1906. He is also known to have been a member of the Berlin Indian Committee or Indian Revolutionary Society which came up in 1914 as a part of the *Gadar* movement. He was also a younger brother of Swami Vivekananda. He wrote his article primarily to dispute the opinion that the burial system was unknown among the people behind the Vedic literature. He showed references to complete inhumations of the dead bodies both in the Rigveda (10.8) and the *Satapatha Brahmana*. He further points out that the *Asvalayana-Grihya-Sutra* discusses the practice of urn burials in detail. It is clearly written that the dead body should be burned first and then the bones should be gathered in an urn and deposited in a pit. Drawing attention to the finds of urn-burials at Harappa, Datta asks: "were these jars containing the bones the same as described in the *Grihya-Sutra*? The location of the discovered site lends further proof of such a possibility. Harappa is situated in the Punjab which has been the homeland of the Vedic Aryans" (Datta 1936: 229). His next step was to undertake an 'anthropological enquiry of Indus valley people: past and present'. In this section he discusses the problem of racial categories of the Indian population and objects to the idea that the Indus civilization people could not be the Vedic Aryans because "no skull of dolichocephal-leptorrhine, tall-statured and blond variety of men has been discovered in these remains". The idea of equating such a group of people to the Indo-Europeans is called the Nordic or Proto-Nordic hypothesis. He points out that the Germany of post-Versailles treaty made Nordicism the basis of its socio-political chauvinism. And this chauvinism of Germany has long ago been taken up by the other Germanic-speaking nations of Europe and America. It has become the political shibboleth of the occidental nations, speaking Teutonic or Germanic languages. The racial chauvinism of Germany has long been taken up by England and America. And today it is intertwined with the chauvinistic outlook of the Germanic-speaking imperialistic nations (Datta 1936: 238).

He then undertakes a tour of the various anthropological theories regarding the racial type of the Indo-Europeans and concludes that we should not "bewail the absence of the dolichocephalic-leptorrhine skulls" in the remains of the Indus civilization. The occurrence of brachycephalic-leptorrhine skulls both at Mohenjodaro and Harappa should be enough, because according to "the French school of Broca, and that of Sergi, it was the brachycephalic Euroasiatics that were the carriers of the Indo-European language to Europe. In that case, they could have been the carriers of Indo-Europeanism to India as well. This will sound a heresy in India where, strangely enough, Germanism is the accredited hypothesis" (Datta 1936: 245-246).

He goes on to argue that,

> we have no right to identify a particular biotype with the Vedic Aryans. If the unbiased opinion of the European savants is that the original Indo-European-speaking people cannot be identified with a people with a particular head-form, likewise we have no right to identify the Vedic Aryans with a particular biotype (Datta 1936-37: 247).

His comments on the Indian literature on this theme are interesting:

> In the field of anthropology, 'Germanism' reigns supreme in India. The Indians being intellectually isolated from the rest of the cultural world, and seeing the outside world only through the English language, have accepted the views of the 'Master' people as the only truth. We have already seen that 'Germanism' as an intellectual tool of imperialism has long been accepted by the Germanic-speaking imperialist countries. And we glory in it because it is the gift of the 'Master' people. The slave-psychology of the Indian mind is reflected in the attempt to prove that the Vedic Aryans were Nordics and in the attempt to ransack the latter-day Sanskrit literature for the proofs of Nordic characteristics (Datta 1936: 247-248).

Datta undertakes a long examination of the relevant Vedic literature and proves that there was nothing in the texts to argue that the Vedic people were blond-haired Nordics. According to him, it is probable that they were of heterogeneous composition as the prehistoric and present-day anthropological data of the Punjab testify. Taking everything into consideration, he argues that there are no valid anthropological objections to the Indus civilization people being Indo-Aryans.

In the third section of his paper Datta undertakes a detailed comparison between the Indus civilization funerary data and the

Vedic funeral customs. On the three types of burials in the Indus civilization – complete burials, fractional burials and post-cremation burials – he cites a wide range of textual data from the Rigveda to the *Grihya-Sutras*, and concludes that there is an agreement between the funeral customs of the Indus civilization and those of the Indo-Aryans.

The next major point Datta raises relates to the characterisation of the Vedic society as only pastoral and agricultural. Datta disputes this by citing references to palaces (IX.86.41), right of private property (VIII.54-55), a society differentiated in different occupations and a society developing class-distinctions. There are references to guilds and *Sresthis* or the rich merchants. At the end of this section Datta concludes that "the cultural condition of the Vedic Aryans as depicted by Marshall does not find complete support from Vedic literature" and that "the Vedic literature is a vast one which bears witness to different phases of the evolution of the Indo-Aryans and the extent of the period of this evolution is still debatable" (Datta 1937: 4-5).

Datta's marshalling of the argument against accepting the chronology of the Rigveda and the Vedic literature between 1000/1200 BC and 500 BC is very logical and dependent to some extent on that great historian of Sanskrit literature, Maurice Winternitz: "No power on earth can any time be sure whether the Vedic Hymns were composed 1000 or 1500 or 2000 or 3000 years before Christ". Another opinion of Winternitz that he cites is that there is nothing to speak against the acceptance of the hypothesis that the Vedic literature goes back to the third and old Indian culture goes back to the fourth millennium; and the dates of Max Muller in the face of our present knowledge of the political, literary and religious history of ancient India, are no longer tenable. This has been convincingly proved by G. Buhler as well (Datta 1937: 7).

He returns to this theme again, after examining in detail the proposition that the Vedic literature seems to have encompassed a great range of varying socio-economic and ethnological conditions:

> For all these ethnological reasons, the date arbitrarily fixed by some of the Indologists seem to be incorrect and the date of the Veda seems to be far anterior to those assigned by these savants (Datta 1937: 13).

More cultural examinations, especially of the religious traits of the Indus civilization, follow, and his conclusion is that there was much that was common between the religions of the Indus civilization and the Vedic literature.

> All we can say in this matter is that much of the religion of Mohenjodaro was not unknown to the Indo-Aryans of the Vedic age, and there is a continuous link between this religion and the present-day popular Hinduism. Hence, it can be said, that in religious matters, the present-day Hindus are the descendants of the Indus Valley people (Datta 1937: 27).

He then goes on to discuss the theories regarding the date of Indo-European migration, etc. and again points out, on the basis of his firm familiarity with the contemporary literature and its logic, that firm dates in this matter are best avoided.

Datta's essay is marked by cool logic and understanding of how the entire Indo-European problem has shaped up and what were the props on which the hypothesis stands. He sums up the whole issue of the Indus civilization and its relationship, or lack of it, with the Vedic literature in the following terms:

> We think it is probable that the advent of the Indo-Aryans in India took place in a dim period which cannot be ascertained today and that it is far anterior to the date arbitrarily fixed by the Indologists with their bias of Nordicism. By a comparative study we have already seen that much of cultural elements are common between both the groups of people in question here ... Rather on the basis of this comparison, we have reason to believe that the people of the Indus Valley culture and the Vedic Aryans belonged to the same ethnic-cultural group. The modes of the disposal of the dead bear out this fact ... Thus we conclude that the absence of the Indo-Aryans in Mohenjodaro and Indus Valley civilization is not proved; their presence is rather suspected as evinced by the modes of the disposal of the dead, and it is clearly discernible at Harappa (Datta 1937: 68).

Datta's idea that the advent of the Indo-Europeans in India took place in a 'dim period which cannot be ascertained today' was also suggested by H.C. Chakladar who delivered his Presidential address to the Anthropological Section of the Indian Science Congress in its annual session at Indore in January 1936. Taking up the attempt of J.H. Hutton in the Census edited by him in 1931 to prove that the Vedic Aryan culture was introduced in

India by the tall long-headed branch of the Indo-Europeans, Chakladar argues that if one looks at the anthropological data, 'unbiased by the Nordic obsession', the evidence both of anthropology and the Vedic literature show that the Alpine brachycephals played a great, if not a greater share, "in the development and propagation of the Aryan language and of the Vedic religion" (Chakladar 1936: 116). Among other things, he argued that the Alpine brachycephals, the skulls of whom occur at Mohenjodaro, entered India first and were the first immigrants of Aryan speech in the land.

Scholars like Bhupendra Nath Datta and Haran Chandra Chakladar represented in their day the best of anthropological scholarship in India. Among other things, they castigated the racial classificatory systems of Risley and Hutton, both whom liberally used such terms as Aryan and Dravidian to describe Indian physical types. Chakladar points out the various confusions introduced by the use of these terms; for instance, Dravidian of one anthropologist was the pre-Dravidian of another anthropologist. Chakladar also thinks that Hutton 'made confusion worse confounded' by using a fresh designation, 'Proto-Australoid' to denote the primitive people of India. Regarding Risley's Dravidian type, which Risley puts between the Vindhyas and Cape Comorin and between the Aravallis and Rajmahal, he points out that many of these people do not speak languages of the Dravidian family and are different from the Dravidians of south India. Interestingly, Suniti Kumar Chatterji who was a 'comparative philologist' with no critical ability to examine the justification of the various racial terms coined in the Indian context, tried to relate the traditional scheme of language developments in India to the Risley-Hutton schemes.

M.S. Vats admitted in his Harappa report in 1940 that "the connexions or affinities between the Vedic Aryans and the cultures concerned with the Harappa burials are not quite clear" (Vats 1940: 209) but he did not hesitate to analyse the mythology of some Cemetery H pottery paintings in terms "of the rites, rituals, and beliefs contained in hymns 14, 16, and 18 of the Xth Mandala of the Rigveda" and added that "the similarity of beliefs, as far as it goes, is very striking".

The idea of an Aryan invasion to account for the end of the Indus civilization took shape only in 1947 when Mortimer Wheeler in the report on his excavations at Harappa in 1946 reported a fortification wall around the western mound at the site and cited the Rigvedic references to the fort-destroying activities of Indra to argue that the fortified cities of the Indus civilization, such as the one which had existed at Harappa, could be the only fortifications which Indra could destroy, given that the usual accepted date of the Aryan migration to India was 1500 BC. He does not mention if he had taken the Rigvedic references from the 1926 publication of R.P. Chanda; the Archaeological Survey of India 'folklore' has it that his attention to these references was drawn by V.S. Agarwal who was then a trainee excavator in the Survey. An adjunct of this main argument was that there were a few scattered skeletons in the upper levels of Mohenjodaro, which could denote a 'time of trouble', the phase of an external attack. At Harappa the Cemetery H pot burials which succeeded an earlier earth burial cemetery and whose pots were different in shape and painting than the typical Harappan pottery of the earlier cemetery, were supposed to be the archaeological marker of Aryans at the site.

Wheeler's 'Aryan explanation' for the demise of Harappa, and by extension, of the Indus civilization, lingered on for a long time, mainly because of the two books he subsequently wrote – *The Indus Civilization* (1953) and *Early India and Pakistan* (1959) – and their 'hegemonic status' in the Indian university curriculum. The fact that the Mohenjodaro skeletons did not belong to the same level and thus could not denote a single phase happening was pointed out by G.F. Dales in 1964 (Dales 1964), and earlier, B.B. Lal (1953) pointed out that there was a debris deposit between the Harappan burials of Stratum II and the Cemetery H burials of Stratum I, and thus the Cemetery H people could not be held responsible for the invasion of Harappa, even if such an invasion had in fact taken place.

In 1953, the year in which Wheeler published *The Indus Civilization*, P.V. Kane, the famous author of the history of *Dharmasastra* literature and the recipient of *Bharat-Ratna*, the highest national-level award in India, delivered the Presidential Address of the sixteenth session of Indian History Congress at Waltair or modern Visakhapatnam. Two parts of this address are relevant to the present context because they examine the issue of relationship between the Harappan civilization and the Vedic Aryans. First, he takes up the dating of the Rigveda, especially the philological argument that the Avesta, parts of which are akin to the Rigveda, cannot be dated much earlier than 800 BC. On this, his comment is the following:

> The philological argument is quite unreliable; different languages continue to keep intact or develop or change their form and structure in varying periods of time. Supposing the date assigned to the Avesta is correct (about which I have grave doubts) that is no conclusive reason for assigning the same date to a similar language cultivated in a different country and in different environments (Kane 1953: 10).

Secondly, he puts a lot of stress on the chronological implications of some important astronomical references in the Rigveda and the Brahmanical literature. Following him, a summary of these references and their implied chronology may be drawn up here:

(1) The Frog hymn in *RV* VII.103, which indicates that the summer solstice was the beginning of the year (verse 9), and *RV* X.85.13 which shows that the beginning of the year was in *Falguni*; the summer solstice was in *Falguni nakshatra* about 4000 or 4500 BC.

(2) *RV* I.105.11 refers to the heliacal rising of Sirius at the vernal equinox, which leads to a date of about 4500 BC.

(3) The *Taittiriya Samhita*, VII.4.8 states that the Full Moon in *Falguni* marked the beginning of the year, which would imply that the date of that year was 4000 BC; this *TS* section also says that at one time the Full Moon in *Chitra nakshatra* marked the beginning of the year, which in turn would date the year at about 6000 BC.

(4) The *TS*, III.1.1.5 mentions Jupiter confronting or occulting *Tishya*, which suggests a date of c. 4650 BC.

(5) The *Satapatha Brahmana*, II.1.2.2 and 4 suggest that the *Krittikas* did not move and were thus on the Equator, and this has been interpreted to result in a date of 3000 BC.

(6) The texts such as the *TS* IV.4.10, the *Taittiriya Brahmana* 1.5.1 and III.1.2-17,
Atharvaveda XIX.7 and the *Maitrayani Samhita* II.13.20 refer to the early lists of *nakshatras* beginning with *Krittika*; the vernal equinox was in *Krittika* about 2300 BC.

(7) The *Vedanga Jyotisha* of the *RV* (verses 5-7) states that the winter solstice was in *Sravistha*, which may indicate a date of 1400 BC for this observation.

What is important is that according to Kane,

> The cumulative effect of the above-mentioned astronomical observations should far outweigh the purely conjectural and subjective argument of Max-Muller and the so-called philological analogy derived from the supposed date of the Avesta (Kane 1956: 11).

Kane's argument is that the Harappan and Vedic chronologies both being 'quite various, fluid and not generally accepted', arguments of Vedic/Harappan relationship should not be based on chronological considerations.

Interestingly, Kane anticipates a major part of Dales' argument regarding the 'mythical massacres of Mohenjodaro' in 1964. He points out that both Mohenjodaro and Harappa were major cities and that in the event of an Aryan attack, "the remains of dead bodies would have been found on an enormous scale" and would not have been limited to only 26 skeletons at Mohenjodaro. Regarding the cause of desertion of these two cities, he infers that the rivers on the banks of which they stood, possibly shifted way.

Comparing the internal evidence of the Rigveda and the excavated evidence of the Indus settlements, he finds both similarities and dissimilarities. One of the similarities he notes is reverence for water both in the Indus civilization and the Rigveda. Drawing attention to the occurrence of bulls on the Indus seals, he notes that in the Rigveda Indra and other gods are spoken of as *Vrisha* or *Vrishabha* or bull. For instance in *RV* VII.19.1 Indra is called a bellowing sharp-horned bull. Similarly, *Pippala* or *Pipul* tree is venerated both in the Indus and *RV*. Kane then goes into a detailed discussion on the use of the terms *Dasas, Dasyus, Panis,* etc. and concludes that when the Rigveda was being composed, "there were admittedly Aryan people who fought against Aryans as well as dasas or dasyus" (Kane 1953: 16). His final conclusion in this regards is (Kane 1953: 17):

> The above brief discussion may lead one to hold that there is some evidence to believe that the inhabitants of the ancient Indus valley fortified cities were probably Aryans holding different views as to ritual and worship from those of the Rigvedic people or were a dark-skinned race differing from the Rigvedic people but contemporaneous with the Rigveda Aryans, that the culture of these cities is not more ancient than that of the Rigvedic

> people and that the astronomical evidence alluded to above would indicate that the Rigvedic people were earlier than the Indus Valley people. *The evidence being meagre it is best not to dogmatise* (italics added).

The Aryan idea did not certainly go away from the Indian archaeological literature after this; if anything throughout the 1950s and 1960s the idea completely dominated this literature in various forms. B.B. Lal's idea that the Painted Grey Ware conformed to the period of the *Mahabharata* and was an 'Aryan pottery' soon became firmly entrenched in the archaeological studies of the Ganga plain; in north India this was considered almost axiomatic even in the 1990s. However, over the years, especially with the increasing emphasis on the natural forces as the cause of Harappan decline and the evidence of continuity of Harappan occupation in various areas, the Aryan issue may be said to have lost some of its intensity, although one cannot ignore the implications of the finds of fire-altars at various Harappan sites, especially Kalibangan and Lothal, on which a detailed analysis was made by S.R. Rao, the excavator of Lothal, in 1993 (Rao 1993). Rao is also noted for his attempted decipherment of the Indus script, but that is an entirely different issue. Here we are concerned only with Rao's study of the Harappan fire-altars.

Drawing attention to the row of seven fire-altars on top of one of the platforms in the citadel mound of Kalibangan and also to the occurrence of fire-altars in some houses of the 'lower city', Rao argues that the seven fire-altars of Kalibangan may relate to seven types of Vedic Soma sacrifice (*Somayaga*). More important is his explanation of a terracotta cake from Kalibangan, which is engraved with the motif of a horned deity with a twig as the headgear. A man is shown leading an animal on the reverse of the same cake. Rao's explanation is that the animal is being taken for sacrifice to the god who in this case may be *Agni*, because, according to an explanation in the *Satapatha Brahmana*, he is associated with wood and plants.

Similarly, Rao's explanation of an evidence from Lothal deserves notice.

> The sacrificial altar of mud-bricks built in a house in square B 19 of Phase III in the Lower Town of Lothal is a very significant evidence throwing light on the Harappan cult of animal sacrifice.

> The mud-brick enclosure, 2 ft 9 inches x 2 ft 6 inches and 8 inches in height is built over a low platform of mud-bricks. It contains charred mandible of an animal of bovine group beside a gold disc-pendant, a carnelian bead, three potsherds painted in chocolate over buff slip and a large quantity of ash. The altar and enclosure were not disturbed. The mud platform served as a sacrificial altar and the enclosure as a sacrificial pit. The gold pendant resembles the circular objects on the forehead and arm of the statue of a 'priest' from Mohenjodaro. The Rigveda mentions that gold ornaments *nishka* and *rukma* served as ritual ornaments. The presence of potsherds in the Lothal altar is significant for they might have been used for preparing sacrificial cakes. The *Brahmana* literature mentions potsherds of various sizes used for the preparation of sacrificial cakes (*Purodasa*). Gold beads and *nishka* were given as gifts to the priests who participated in the performance of sacrifices during the Vedic period. Perhaps, the Harappan sacrificer, too, offered them (Rao 1993: 175).

The point is not whether Rao is right or wrong in his explanation. The point is that the increasing reports of Harappan fire-altars and their Vedic analogies and even their occurrence in some modern Hindu households make the idea of Vedic-Harappa correlation, as propounded by scholars like B.N. Datta and P.V. Kane more acceptable.

The problem of relationship between the Indus civilization and the Vedas, however, became a focus of concern after the results of the Cholistan archaeological survey were known and it became increasingly clear that there was every reason to argue that the course of the Ghaggar-Hakra in Cholistan denoted possibly the core area of the origin of the Indus civilization. This situation found expression in many Indian archaeological writings including some of mine (cf. Chakrabarti 1997 reprint: 46). S.P. Gupta (1996) gave expression to this when he coined the term 'Indus-Sarasvati civilization'.

This archaeological development could not but lead to a renewed interest in the problem of Indus civilization/Vedas relationship. There is virtually no disagreement with the idea that the Ghaggar-Hakra course denotes the bed of the Sarasvati. The vast extinct drainage system between the Indian Siwaliks and the Rann of Kutch, which took in the Cholistan desert along its course from the Siwaliks to the Rann of Kutch represents the now-extinct course of a river which has been said to be the river of all rivers in the *RV* itself. What happened was that some people became very aware of the significance of the Sarasvati system in Indian archaeology and cultural history. S. Kalyanaraman's massive website on the Sarasvati, regardless of the interpretations and the attitude displayed there, reflects this awareness. It is not that the Vedas are replete with references to this river, nor was it the only river mentioned in the Vedas. But the very facts that the *RV* knew it and that a part of its valley denoted the epicentre of the Indus civilization exercised, quite naturally, a powerful influence on the scholarly imagination.

This must be the primary factor behind a renewed and intense interest not merely in the Sarasvati but also in the Aryan premise as a whole. If one leaves aside the polemical literature coming from various quarters, one notes two trends. First, there are increasing attempts to question the deep-rooted premise that the Rigveda described only an agricultural-cum-pastoral society. Bhagwan Singh's *The Vedic Harappans* which lists, among other things, the technical terms used in the *RV* for warfare, stock-breeding and agriculture, pottery, different crafts and professions, navigation, overland trade and commerce, and – very significantly in the Harappan context – housing and urban centres. R.S. Bisht, the excavator of Dholavira, pointed out in many lectures and discussions that the division of this city into three distinct parts – upper, middle and lower – has clear echoes in the *RV*. As early as 1989-90 he wrote that the three principal divisions of the urban layout of Dholavira in view of their respective location and construction, have been christened as 'citadel' or 'acropolis', 'middle town' and 'lower town', borrowing from the Rigveda (of) three significant terms, viz., *parama*, *madhyama* and *avama*. These terms are frequently used therein to denote three different orders or types of divine or mundane horizons, zones, assemblies or settlements, rather divisions. Importantly, the *Atharvaveda* mentions the occupants of these respective divisions as *paramesthin*, *madhyamesthin* and *avamesthin* (Bisht 1989-90: 72).

The Rigvedic references which Bisht cites are *RV* I.108.6, VI.25.1, X.81.5. In 1988 he argued strongly in favour of the idea that the arts of navigation and both overland and maritime trade were clearly known to the *RV*.

> Significantly, there are a few terms which became during the historical times expressly connected with business transactions. They are: *artha* (VII.63.4; X.29.5) for wealth; *avyaya* (VIII.86.2) for capital investment; *bhaga* (VIII.86.2, VIII.79.6; X.11.8; VIII.36.6) for share that is contributed towards investment, or obtained as profit; *gratha* (VII.6.3) for capital invested in business; *rina* (VIII.47.17) for loan; *sulka* (VII.82.6; VIII.1.5) for custom or octroi tax; *bali* (VIII.89.9) for tribute to superior authority, king or god; *suvita* (V.80.3) and *vitta* (VII.42.2) for wealth or money; *samvidana* for agreement or contract between two parties; *vasna* for value or cost (IV.24.9) or for wealth or merchandise (VI.47.21) (Bisht 1988).

Considering that the *RV*, as argued by P.V. Kane, belongs to a wide period and contains in all likelihood different economic frameworks of different periods, the references collected by Bisht or Singh and their interpretations offered by them need not cause surprise. The historiography of how the different Vedic terms have been interpreted by various scholars since the beginning of academic Vedic studies deserves possibly a detailed study in its own right. There is no reason to believe that the interpretations given by scholars like Bisht and Singh are in any way less trustworthy than the agricultural-pastoral interpretation of the Rigvedic society by other scholars. An interesting development is M. Danino's argument that the various ratios of measurements adopted for the city planning of Dholavira continue in the later measuring traditions of texts like the *Shulba Sutras* (Danino 2004-2005). He developed his argument on the basis of Bisht's calculation of measurements of the various components of the Dholavira settlement (Bisht 1998-99).

The second offshoot of the increasing concern with the Sarasvati is B.B. Lal's examination of the 'Aryan homeland' (Lal 2005). Beginning with the archaeologist G. Possehl's opinion (Possehl 1996: 65) that the Rigveda mentions trees of the cold climatic region such as birch, scotch pine, linden, alder and oak, Lal points out that none of these trees found any mention in the *RV*; on the contrary, there are references to such Indian trees as *Asvattha (Ficus religiosa), Kimsuka (Butea monosperma), Khadira (Acacia catechu), Nyagrodha (banyan tree, Ficus Bengalensis L), Vibhidaka (Terminalia bellerica or bahera), Salmali (silk cotton tree)* and *Simsapa (Dalbergia sissoo)*. He also puts up a similar list of subcontinental plants and grasses. The list of the *RV* fauna drawn up by him includes many subcontinental items including water buffalo, peacock and *Chakravaka*. Among other things, he points out the occurrence of spoked wheel in the mature Harappan level of Rakhigarhi and the terracotta figure of a horse in the same level at Lothal. Regarding the chronological position of the *RV* his position is the following:

> ... since during the Rigvedic times the Sarasvati was a mighty flowing river and according to the archaeological-radio-carbon-dating-cum-hydrological evidence this river dried around 2000 BC, the *Rigveda has got to be earlier than 2000 BC*. How much earlier, it would, of course, be anybody's guess (Lal 2005: 13).

He goes on to write,

> Further, since the *Rigveda* must be dated to a period prior to 2000 BC, a question may straightaway be posed: which archaeological culture covered the entire region from the Ganga on the east to the Indus on the west during the period prior to 2000 BC? Please think coolly and dispassionately. If you do that, you cannot escape the inevitable conclusion: *it was none other than the Harappan civilization itself.* However, in spite of such strong evidence in support of a Vedic+Harappan equation, it would be prudent, as I have all along advocated, to put this equation on hold until the Harappan script is satisfactorily deciphered (Lal 2005: 14-15).

It may be pointed out here that Iravatham Mahadevan worked out a correlation between the Indus civilization and the Rigveda in the early 1980s on the basis of his logical and clear argument that the trough in front of the unicorn on Harappan seals was a filter to process the pressing of Soma, the ubiquitous Rigvedic drink (Mahadevan 1984).

At the same time, it has to be admitted that not all scholars have taken kindly to the idea of Harappa-Vedic equation. R.S. Sharma (1999: 77) writes that the pastoralists of the Bactro-Margiana culture complex came to India and this migration resulted in the genesis of the Rigveda. There are also scholars who cannot accept that horse was known to the Harappas.

Whatever may be the areas of scholarly agreements or disagreements, there is no doubt that the initial assumption of the pre- and non-Vedic status of the Indus civilization has been questioned right from the beginning, and the scholars involved in this process of questioning, beginning with R.P. Chanda who postulated, in fact, a phase of interaction between the Harappans and the 'Vedic Aryans', were people well-rooted both in the texts and the archaeological data. The history of the idea might not have been strong or forceful all along, and the reason why this has assumed some sharpness today is mainly due to the fact that the Sarasvati has emerged as the focal area of origin of the Indus civilization. No credit goes to the scholars who prefer to put it in the Helmand basin. Among other things, B.B. Lal (2005) has cited *RV* references to the facts that this river lay between the Yamuna and the Sutlej, had *Drishadvati* and *Apaya* as tributaries, and flowed all the way from the mountains to the sea. Archaeologically, no credence need be attached to R.S. Sharma's opinion that the BMAC culture migrated to India and that the *RV* reflects this migration. Regarding horse, there is no reason to stick to the opinion of those who believe that horse was unknown to the Harappans. Even without going into the fact that horse-bones have been identified both in and before the Harappan contexts by highly competent professionals including B. Nath of the Zoological Survey of India, the Harappans could easily have imported horses from central Asia at the border of which they had their site Shortughai. Traditionally, India has never been a horse-breeding area, and in the historical periods one of the major supply zones was central Asia. One fails to understand why the Harappan situation had to be fundamentally different.

However, the implication of Lal's argument that the Rigveda, as the list of its flora and fauna shows, was composed in the Indian soil, is not clear. Does he believe that there were people who can be called Aryans and that they migrated elsewhere from India?

VIII. MORE ON THE DRAVIDIAN PREMISE OR THE QUESTION OF THE DRAVIDIAN AUTHORSHIP OF THE INDUS CIVILIZATION

Although better known under the rubric of 'Dravidian authorship', the question is basically that of Tamilian authorship of this civilization. In an epigraphical study R. Nagaswamy (1993) has demonstrated how the epigraphic evidence from the 3rd/2nd century BC to c. ninth century AD in Orissa, Andhra, Karnataka, Tamil Nadu and Sri Lanka is consistent in showing that "the term *Dramida* or *Dravida* stood for *Tamil*, so far as ancient Indians are concerned".

This particular authorship issue is wholly dependent on certain hypotheses regarding India's language and 'racial' history which was in place by the early years of the twentieth century. According to H. Risley, the main exponent of India's racial scheme of the period, there was a pure 'Dravidian type' of race typified by the Paniyans of south Indian hills and the Santals of east India. In his scheme of things, he was the original inhabitant of India, recognizable by his dark skin colour, squat figure and the 'Negro-like' proportions of his nose. He was also given the status of being archetypal Indian 'coolie'. However, there were also three mixed Dravidian types: the Scytho-Dravidian (Maratha Brahmins, Kunbis and Coorgs of western India), the Aryo-Dravidian (Uttar Pradesh, parts of Bihar, Rajputana and Sri Lanka) and the Mongolo-Dravidian (Bengali Brahmins and Kayasthas, East Bengal Muslims, and other regional groups). The language-history of the period rested on G. Grierson's report on languages in the census of 1901. He had no hesitation in accepting the Brahui tongue of Baluchistan as a member of the Dravidian family of languages which, apart from the obvious major languages such as Tamil, Kanarese, Telugu and Malayalam, contained some minor languages and constituted a total of twenty-six. The Brahuis did not display Dravidian ethnic characteristics but spoke undoubtedly a Dravidian language. The Dravidians who were in the north became 'Aryanized' but retained their ethnic characteristics.

The notion of a developed Dravidian culture independent of Indo-Aryan culture goes back to 1856 when Bishop P. Caldwell worked out this idea on the basis of pure Dravidian words. Thus the premises, which were in the background of the Dravidian authorship idea propounded by R.D. Banerji and S.K. Chatterji, almost simultaneously with the discovery of the Indus civilization were the following: the Dravidian language was once widespread in north India as far west as Baluchistan; if it lay confined to the southern Peninsula and a few areas to the northeast of this peninsula, that was because its speakers were slowly forced to their present distribution by the inroads of the speakers of the Indo-Aryan language family. Thirdly, the Dravidians, as their language analysis revealed, were the bearers of a developed culture.

In the 1930s, in J.H. Hutton's racial scheme for India, the 'Proto-Australoids' came first to India from the western direction and were followed by an early branch of the Mediterranean race which also brought in agriculture. There was also a later migration of the civilized Mediterraneans who introduced metals but not iron. Still later, there were dolichocephalic Mediterranean immigrants with advanced culture, but there was also an element of the Armenoid brachycephalic branch of the Alpine race, and out of this amalgam was created the Indus civilization. Again, two points deserve notice: a link between the Mediterraneans and the Dravidians, and the rise of the Indus civilization as a result of the dolichocephalic Mediterranean and brachycephalic Armenoid Alpine. In retrospect, the Mediterranean link of the Dravidian origins got entrenched, and a whole lot of related ideas soon took over the Dravidian scene. Only one example will suffice in the present context. V. Ramachandra Dikshitar's *Origin and Spread of the Tamils*, although published only in 1947, were given as lectures to Madras University in November 1940. Accepting the idea of Lemuria, a so-called geological bridge linking India and Africa at the end of the Mesozoic era, he argues that south India must have had "pre-Palaeolithic people who were the aboriginals and sons of the soil" (Dikshitar 1947: 3). After a long and tenuous argument he goes on to write that the ethnic type of the Sumerians and of the Indus valley people was the south Indian type, and that "there is every reason of a migration of the Indus people from Indus valley to Dravida and from Dravida to the Indus valley".

In arguments of this kind, basically it is faith and conviction which matter. Academic reasoning is not at all an issue in such cases; if no straightforward logic is forthcoming, recourse can always be taken to the tortuous dark alleys of philological and racial scholarship. In the case of the Indus civilization's Dravidian premise, this is exactly what happened early on in the history of its scholarship.

It is clear from Sumathi Ramaswami's (Ramaswamy 2001) and Michael Burgander's (Burgander 2004) essays that the Tamil nationalism of the period was ready to accept this Dravidian premise of the Indus civilization with a lot of enthusiasm. One has to put aside here the various decipherment schemes which assume that the Harappans were speaking a language of the Dravidian family, just as we have previously set aside all such attempts based on the Indo-Aryan premise.

Socio-politically, the Indo-Aryan premise of the Indus civilization or just the premise itself was not acceptable to a vast majority of Indians. B.R. Ambedkar's hostility to the notion is well-known, and if anything, the idea of the Indo-Aryan invaders subjugating the numerically dominant autochthones and putting them at the lower end of the caste hierarchy could not have been acceptable to any social reformer concerned with the plight of the *Dalits* in Ambedkar's time or earlier. Bergunder (2004: 63) lays stress on the role of Jyotiba Phule (1827-1890) in emphasizing this attitude; he had no patience for "the Aryan progenitors of the present Brahmin race", who were not the aborigines of India but came from beyond the Hindukush. The establishment of the Aryan domination and supremacy over the subjugated aboriginals was something to be loathed, and escape from, through conversions to Buddhism. By the end of the nineteenth century, neo-Buddhism had made its base in western India.

It is the status as the creators of the first civilization of India which appealed to Tamil nationalism. Indigenousness was not an issue here, because the Tamils were laying claim to the Tamil links of various areas and peoples extending up to the Mediterranean. Ramaswamy cites the incident of putting forward an individual Dravida Munnetra Kazagham (DMK) member's resolution in the Tamil Nadu legislative assembly in August 1970, whereby the member sought the appointment of a board of scholars to put at rest once and for all any controversy regarding the idea that the Indus civilization was a creation of the Tamil people. No undue emphasis should be given to such erratic behaviour on the part of a lone MLA of the Tamil Nadu assembly; our legislative assemblies have always had the distinction of being peopled by some colourful and interesting legislators. However, it is not possible to ignore Ramaswamy's summing-up of the overall ideological situation:

> Tamil nationalist intellectuals, however, do more than just name and claim the Indus valley remains as 'Tamil'. From 1927 onwards, they have also argued that these remains offer unquestionable *material* proof of the existence of Dravidian/ Tamil culture all over India, and of the 'civilized' status of Tamil speakers from distant antiquity. They find proof in the remains of all manner of cultural forms that have been deemed authentically Tamil, such as the worship of Siva or verses from the *Tirukkural*. They note that the language of the Indus peoples could have been none other than Tamil, and that any modern speaker of Tamil can with ease understand the script that has

> bedevilled professional attempts at decipherment. Most crucially, they insist that the end of the Indus cities, and of the flourishing Tamil civilization there was caused by the Aryan 'invaders'. So, in their narratives, the Aryans are reduced to being the barbaric destroyers of India's first 'civilization', rather than exalted as being its founders (Ramaswamy 2001: 119)

What is academically somewhat curious is that at no point was it necessary to produce any material evidence in support of the Dravidian premise; the prevalent framework of India's language history and random opinions such as the one of H.R. Hall that the ancient Sumerians could well be a branch of the "Primitive Dravidians from the Indus valley" (Chatterji 1924: 673-674) were considered reasonable enough grounds to prove the validity of the suggested Dravidian authorship of the Indus civilization.

In recent years there has been some attempt to 'discover' archaeological evidence in this regard. In an article called "Harappa and Tamil Culture", S. Gurumurthy, Professor of Archaeology in Madras University, traced archaeological similarities between the two:

1. Globular or pyriform urns with *graffiti*
2. Megalithic burials
3. Ring wells (from Kanchipuram excavations)
4. Huge bricks measuring 18 in x 13 in x 3 in (from Kanchipuram excavations)
5. Mother goddesss terracotta figures (made and shown below the bust only from Tirukkampuliyur excavations)
6. Bronze vessels (from Adichchanallur) (now at Madras Government Museum)
7. Semi-precious stone beads – round, barrel-shaped and etched beads (from all over Tamil Nadu)
8. Bronze figure of a lady with peculiar head-dress (from Adichchanallur) recalls not only Harappan but also pre-Harappan from Pakistan
9. Multiple pots (from Nilgiris megalithic – now at Madras Government Museum)
10. The following vessel types – ringstones, dish-on-stand, incense burner (Thirukkampuliyur), goblet, *lota*, etc.
11. The following graffiti appearing as letters both in the Harappan script and Brahmi

12. The skulls from Adichchanallur represent Mediterranean race and bear close resemblance to Harappan skulls (Gurumurthy 1997: INTAMM website)

The above list is completely misleading. To take up only one case, 'ring wells' occur at Kanchipuram but not at any Harappan site. The Harappan wells are normal brick-lined shaft wells; they are in no case ring wells where terracotta rings are used to line the shaft. Besides, Kanchipuram is an early historic site. One does not compare the materials of a Bronze Age civilization with the materials of an early historic site.

It is possible that to some extent the easy acceptance of materially unverifiable ideas was related to the internal conflicts of the Tamil society of the period. Bergunder (2004) has shown how the Tamil view of history was dominated by the idea that the Aryan-Brahmanical culture brought about in Tamil Nadu by the Brahmin migrations was superior to the Tamil culture which prevailed locally. He cites an author – Srinivasa Aiyangar – who wrote as late as 1914:

> ... it is evident that the whole Tamil literature is permeated with Aryan influence and that practically there was no literature worth the name among the Tamils before the migration of Brahmans to south India (Bergunder 2004: 78).

This attitude led to a sharp reaction from the Tamil neo-Saiva movement of the late nineteenth and early twentieth centuries. The Brahmanical view of Tamil history was contradicted and

> ... a complex model of Tamil superiority was developed around the claim that the Tamils were the original inhabitants of the Indian subcontinent. Contrary to the Brahmanical view of history, the neo-Saivites held that the numerically few immigrant Aryans were entirely without culture and owed their own linguistic, cultural and religious traditions entirely to contact with the advanced Tamil culture. With this argument they also defended themselves against a Brahmanical Hinduism which classified them as Sudras (Bergunder 2004: 78-79).

Bergunder also draws attention to the attitudes of the Dravidian movement in relation to the Aryan/Dravidian dichotomy. The secular Dravidian movement took its political form first in the formation of the Justice Party or South Indian Liberal Federation in 1916, which was dominated by the richer section of the non-

Brahmin castes – the Chettis and Vellalars. In 1925 E.V. Ramaswami Naicker, also known as Periyar (1879-1973), started the Self-Respect movement which had as its aims the protest against Brahmanical caste-oppression and a new model of the Tamilian past and society.

> We do not need to explain how the Aryans entered and settled in the Dravidian country ... and subjugated and oppressed the Dravidians. Nor do we need to explain how before the Aryans entered the Dravidian country, the Dravidian country had a civilization and arts of the highest rank (Ramaswami cited by Bergunder 2004: 81).

To Ramaswami, the Indus civilization was the Dravidian (Tamilian) creation, and even to Bharathi Dasan (1891-1964), the great Tamil poet, the Aryans were nothing but plunderers.

The idea was also taken up by C.N. Annadurai who took over the reins of the Dravidian movement from Ramaswami:

> When the European researchers fabricated and promulgated the fiction according to which the Aryans are supposed violently to have invaded and to have brought culture to the people, these high-caste people began jealously to support this fiction, for it fed their pride (Annadurai cited by Bergunder 2004: 83).

What comes though very clearly in the examination of the Dravidian premise is that it is much more than a mere academic debate. The aspirations of the vast non-Brahmin Tamil communities came to be intimately linked with this.

It is also to the credit of Bergunder to point out that the Aryan invasion idea was viewed in its own way by the various *Dalit* movements, especially the *Adi Hindu* and *Adi Dharam* movements, both of which developed primarily in the 1920s. One of their cardinal tenets was that they were the original owners of the land and the Aryans mere aggressors and oppressors. In Bergunder's analysis, the 'Hindu nationalists' personified by such persons as V.D. Savarkar and M.S. Golwalkar, the theoretical exponents of the RSS movement, came to believe that the idea that the Aryans came from outside was a myth; they were indigenous to India and provide Hinduism with a continuous history in the land. As far as one has been able to determine, there is no direct connection between the Indus civilization and the Vedic literature, according to these analysts.

Finally, it is important to stress that the question of Aryan/Dravidian authorship of the Indus civilization has been with us since the discovery of this civilization. Specific correlations between the Vedic literature and this civilization have been worked out by various scholars including B.N. Datta and P.V. Kane, and we have seen how and why this trend has emerged into sharp focus in recent years. The Dravidian theory has been based mostly on the early reconstruction of India's language and racial histories and got inextricably mixed with caste-conflicts in Tamil Nadu. Both these approaches continue to remain forceful.

IX. THE CURRENT POLITICS OF THE INDUS CIVILIZATION STUDIES

1. The Aryan/Dravidian Debate

We have followed the essential historical development of this debate in the preceding section. We have seen that the Dravidian side of it got tied with the neo-Saivite and 'Dravidian' movements. However, when earlier scholars like R.D. Banerji or S.K. Chatterji were putting forward the idea of the Indus civilization being a creation of the Dravidians in general and of the Tamils in particular, they had no particular political axe to grind. Their ideas simply imply that they accepted the historical framework of the Indian 'races' and languages, which came to them with various modifications from the late nineteenth century and later. To the Indian nationalists of the day, all the language groups of the country contributed in various ways to the formation of the Indian culture which to them was like a bouquet of flowers. However much I disagree with Chatterji's approach to the Indian past or Banerji's enunciation of various 'islands' at the site of Mohenjodaro, I cannot for a moment claim that they expressed those ideas for any political consideration. When scholars like Iravatham Mahadevan try to decipher the Indus script assuming that the language concerned belonged to the Dravidian family of languages, I cannot think that he is doing so because his mother-tongue is Tamil.

On the other hand, the scholars who criticized the Dravidian idea did not suffer from any sense of antagonism to the modern Tamils. This is what P.V. Kane wrote on this idea:

> The word Dravida itself does not occur, as so far known, in any work or inscription that can be assigned to an earlier date than the 1st or 2nd century BC .... The only plausible ground urged is that the Brahuis of Baluchistan speak a language akin to Dravidian speech. The Brahuis are a mere oasis in a desert and even in these days the population of Brahuis in Baluchistan and Sind is about two hundred thousand. The Brahuis point to Aleppo as their ancestral home, and theirs is not a written language ... the Brahuis are ... but a medley of peoples inheriting diverse traditions and customs. It is now generally admitted that persons now speaking the same language are not necessarily of the same stock. From the mere fact that the structure of the Brahui speech is akin to Dravidian, it does not follow that the Brahuis and Dravidians belong to the same racial stock nor does it follow that because the Brahuis are near the Indus Valley sites the people who inhabited those cities were Dravidians. If the Dravidians had been pushed southwards more than 1000 miles from Baluchistan some vestiges of Dravidian habitations should have been found in North and Central India (Kane 1953: 17-18).

Kane's arguments are clear enough, and one cannot blame him for putting them forward. One also feels that the notion of Aryan/ Dravidian dichotomy has been carried forward to unreasonable proportion these days. Whether this was true in the ancient context seems to be doubtful. Scholars have pointed out that there are copious references to the Vedic rites, *mantras* and Brahmins in the corpus of the Tamil Sangam literature. For instance, Tholkappiar, the author of the earliest extant Tamil grammatical work, was well-versed in Sanskrit grammar (Rangarajan 1993). Other scholars have pointed out that the Tamil term *Ariyar*, or Sanskrit *Arya*, although used in various contexts generally relating to people from beyond the north of *Tamilagam*, have not had the connotation of being foreigners (Ramakrishnarao 1993). The historical stages by which the idea of Aryan/Dravidian dichotomy has developed since the mid-nineteenth century may deserve detailed commentary from scholars who are competent to handle this theme.

Bergunder (2004) seems to be one of the few scholars who have tried to analyse the links of the Aryan idea in the Indus context with reference to the ideas of 'Hindu nationalism' beginning with those of V.D. Savarkar (1893-1966) who apparently had no problem with the idea of Aryan migration to India. He cites M.S. Golwalkar

(1906-1973), a leader of the Rashtriya Svayamsevak Sangha (RSS), writing in 1940 that the "Hindus came into this land from nowhere, but are indigenous children of the soil always, from times immemorial". In Bergunder's analysis this premise – and by implication, the denial of the Aryan invasion theory which assumes that Hinduism was a creation of the migrant Aryans – remained in limbo till the Bharatiya Janata Party (BJP; former 'Janasangha'), RSS and Visva Hindu Parishad, or all the three arms of what is called 'Sangh Parivar', became politically powerful in the 1980s.

As long as one is simply content by claiming that Hinduism is indigenous to India – and even the most diehard critic of Hinduism and all that stands for cannot deny this – there is no problem with this thesis, irrespective of the political beliefs of the persons it springs from. It does not necessarily follow from this that India belongs only to the Hindus! One hopes that not many Hindus are lunatic or intolerant enough to claim this. The point is that the denial of the Aryan invasion theory is not, academically or otherwise, an act of Hindu fundamentalism, and similarly, the idea that there was a relationship between the Indus civilization and the Vedic literature cannot in any way be construed as this. For instance, the parallels between the Harappan mode of the disposal of the dead and the methods of burials described in the Vedic literature have been brought out by several impeccable scholars. If the old image of the Rigvedic society as being only pastoral and agricultural is being supplemented/replaced by the image of a developed society with knowledge of urban designs, that is not because the scholars involved in bringing about this change do not know their Vedic Sanskrit or the possible range of interpretation of the relevant terms but because they feel that the old pastoral-agricultural image does not do this literature justice, so to speak. I find no special virtue in making such laughable statements as that the Rigveda mentions trees of the cold climatic regions or that the Sarasvati has to be located in the Helmand region of Afghanistan.

A scholar (and also a Sanskritist) of the stature of P.V. Kane had no difficulty in acknowledging the implications of the chronological computations of the various astronomical events described in the various segments of the Vedic literature. His opinion that the long time-span of the Vedic literature from the 6th to the 3rd millennia BC and later, that one gets from the calculation of astronomical events mentioned in this literature has to be given more credence than any subjective philological dating is certainly not the opinion of a 'Hindu fundamentalist' *Bharat Ratna*. This system of dating is still considered for dating in the context of ancient Egypt, among other places (cf. Spence 2000), and should not be brushed away with impatience. Personally, my reading of how the Aryan idea has developed its importance in the study of ancient India and how the idea itself formed a keystone of the race-language-culture based approach to history makes me feel convinced that the Aryan idea, as Leon Poliakov (1996) argued before me, is nothing but a racist myth. I cannot comment on the soundness or otherwise of the basic linguistic premises built around it, but I do know that 'comparative philology'/'historical linguistics'/'linguistic palaeontology' has essentially put forward unverifiable or untestable arguments and that there is absolutely no reason why archaeology should consider its own testimony incomplete unless it fits into a plainly hypothetical linguistic framework. More recently Stefan Arvidsson (2006) has traced how the notions of 'Indo-European' and 'Aryan' have been shaped by, and used for, various ideological interests.

However, if I am asked to select, archaeologically, the most probable period of possibly extensive migration of people from the Indo-Iranian borderlands and beyond to the subcontinent, I would unhesitatingly put my finger on the period of the growth of agricultural communities of Baluchistan. I cannot pass over the fact that in the 5th millennium BC and presumably earlier context of Rana Ghundai II in the Zhob valley the pottery forms are clearly identical with the forms of early Sialk and Hissar. The identity is so close, despite some variations in designs, that some movements of people from the direction of Hissar in northeast Iran and Sialk in western Iran need not be denied. I believe I have argued in this line in a publication dated 1986 (Chakrabarti 1986). So, Kane's supposition based on astronomical method of dating does not surprise me, especially when it is good common sense to view the corpus of the Vedic literature as the product of a long period of development in the subcontinent itself. After all, there is nothing in this literature itself, which suggests that it was composed somewhere outside the subcontinent.

In this connection, one has to remember not merely Kane but also scholars like R.P. Chanda who spoke of a period of coexistence and acculturation between the Indus civilization and the Vedic people and B.N. Datta who first noted the similarities between the Vedic and the Indus civilization methods of the disposal of the dead. The name of R.P. Chanda is well known in the Indian archaeological circle; B.N. Datta, the youngest and the second brother of Swami Vivekananda, is possibly less known, but those who may harbour any thought about his being a Hindu fundamentalist may be reminded that he sent at least one of his books to V. Lenin and was recognized later in Calcutta as a socialist/communist/Marxist. What I am trying to convey is that the idea of a Veda-Indus correlation does not necessarily make one a 'Hindu fundamentalist'. This idea has been with us for more than 80 years.

The argument that this idea denotes Hindu fundamentalism or that it is 'anti-Dravidian', as Irfan Habib called it, is a recent phenomenon. One of the strongest expressions that I know of this argument was provided by Romila Thapar in her introduction to the controversy created by N. Rajaram's claim of horse on an Indus seal. I am not concerned with how Rajaram reached his conclusion – by some kind of fraud or not. Acts of fraud, although disguised in different ways, are possibly on the increase in ancient Indian studies. In this case, the presence of horse at Harappa would not surprise me at all; first, horse-bones have been identified in various Harappan contexts by people as competent as the one who figures as the expert in the identification of horse-bones in the articles for which Thapar writes her 'cover story', and second, there is no reason why some horses could not come to the Harappan zone from across the Hindukush passes, just as they are known to have come to the Gangetic plain in the historical period. It is somewhat bizarre that the claim of horse at Harappa should send people into tizzy about the march of 'Hindu fundamentalism'.

Thapar wrote her piece in 2000 when the Indian Council of Historical Research (ICHR) was under the BJP control. The new 'council members' of the ICHR took cue from the members who were there before the BJP came, and used it mostly for the benefit of themselves and their fellow-travellers. However, it was quite natural that the dislodged power group, of which Thapar was a member, should use every opportunity to decry the present leadership, and which intellectual weapon is more popular in India than making things appear as a struggle between 'secularism' and 'fundamentalism/communalism'? This was exactly what Thapar tried to do in her article. It must be remembered that the fight for the control of the ICHR is basically a fight for the control of the entire framework of historical studies in India. This power-tussle is also to gain dominance in the selection committees for various History jobs in various Indian colleges and universities, offering great opportunities to the overlords among the historians to oblige their followers. If this smacks of criminalisation of this section of the Indian academia, one need not be surprised; criminalisation of the history sector of Indian higher education has been a constant feature since the 1970s. This is no longer specific to any political group, but may with some justification trace its roots from the setting up, by the left, of a specific central body, i.e., the ICHR, for the control of the type of research Indian historians will be expected to do. The debate about the Aryan/Dravidian affiliation of the Indus civilization is not, as we have seen, a political debate, but the controversy about the implication of its suggested Aryan affiliation is both comparatively recent and political.

2. The Issue of Name

The distribution of this civilization is in no way limited to the Indus valley, and there is not even a faint justification to go on calling it 'Indus valley civilization', although the term had been sporadically used after the civilization was discovered. In his definitive publication Marshall called it 'the Indus civilization' which is not a logical term in view of its present extension but has the advantage of a long usage. The term 'Indus-Sarasvati civilization' may do justice to the tremendously significant role of the Sarasvati in the genesis of the civilization, but still, it does not connote the whole territory. The neutral term is 'Harappan civilization'. I use this term along with the old term 'Indus civilization'.

The continued use of *Indus valley civilization* is in no way justifiable. In the current political situation it has a clear sub-text. It means that the civilization is the product of the Indus valley in Pakistan and gives the term a firm twist towards Pakistan. One can ignore the frequent occurrence of this term in many Indian publications including the Bulletin of the Indian Archaeological Society *Puratattva*. I am told that in India this term is the literal translation of what people have been reading about since they were young: *Sindhu Ghati ki Sabhyata* ('civilization of the Indus valley'). Its continuous use also shows that the Indian understanding of the politics of the past is still marginal.

When a professional archaeologist uses the term *Indus Valley Civilization* in the title of his book, that cannot be put down to the author's ignorance (Kenoyer 1998). That J.M. Kenoyer would like to give a Pakistan twist to the study of the Harappan civilization is understandable. In an interview with a representative of the American magazine *Archaeology*, he said the following:

> There are various statements in the Koran that say "look at the ruined mounds, see what happened to those who lived in the past, understand the past". This is a guiding principle for some Pakistani archaeologists, though Pakistan is a secular country, and other researchers take a purely scientific approach (Kenoyer 2002: 21).

We are not sure if the citizens of Pakistan themselves would think of themselves as citizens of a 'secular country'. Its 1973 constitution uses the term 'Islamic Republic of Pakistan' and declares that it is a 'State based on Islamic principles of social justice and that "a person shall not be qualified for election as President unless he is a Muslim ...." What is interesting is that Kenoyer thinks it is a 'secular state'.

There is another implication of Kenoyer's Pakistan angle to the study of the Indus civilization. There are archaeologists – and Kenoyer is among them – who like to view the Harappan civilization as the product of an arrow-line of development beginning with Mehrgarh in Baluchistan. G.L. Possehl, for instance, repeatedly draws attention to the importance in this context of what he calls "the middle Asian interaction sphere" between the Gulf and central Asia on the one hand and between the Indus and the Mediterranean on the other. In Chapter 2 of his *Ancient Cities of the Indus Valley Civilization* Kenoyer begins to trace the origins of the Harappan urban society back to Mehrgarh. This approach is in direct contradiction to my approach, i.e., to see the Harappan development as the product of a multilineal agricultural development and interaction with its core area in a limited portion of the Sarasvati valley in the Cholistan area. If the focus of the name is exclusively on the Indus valley, that can easily be linked to the idea that the Harappan civilization was something that can be visualized as beginning with cultural developments in 'middle Asia'. From whichever way we view it, the term *Indus Valley Civilization*, when used by archaeologists like Kenoyer, is a wilful way to downplay, in the study of its genesis and development, the role of those areas which are now parts of the territory of modern India. The fact that the term occasionally finds mention in *Puratattva* only shows how careless some Indian archaeologists can be.

3. The Issue of Origin

Historically, the first major scholar who propagated the idea of an 'alien domination' in the Harappan citadel was Mortimer Wheeler in 1953. The reason why he did so is not clear; my feeling is that he found no reason to encourage the idea of an independent beginning of Bronze Age urban life in India after she was made free of the British rule and became a part of the Third World. My feeling is conditioned to some extent by the reading of Wheeler's *Flames over Persepolis* (Wheeler 1968) which deals with the possible cultural effects of the burning of the Achaemenid capital Persepolis at the hands of the Greeks under Alexander in the East including India. In a sense, the story is also that of the passing away of an empire, leaving behind only major cultural waves, and the shadow of the modern story of the British empire passing away in Wheeler's lifetime was possibly never far from the pages of this book. If one remembers correctly, K.N. Sastri, the long-time curator of the Archaeological Survey of India museum at Harappa, felt that Harappa itself had a much longer pre-Harappan antecedence than Wheeler anticipated and argued for. Sastri's opinion was not taken seriously. As is well-known, the continuing researches in Baluchistan, Sind, and Rajasthan highlighted the long story of Harappan origins by the1960s and in this, the early analyses by W. Fairservis, G. Dales and A. Ghosh played a major role. Since then, the sequence of growth has been detailed in various areas, amply vindicating Marshall's assumption that this civilization is deeply rooted in the Indian soil.

It is not that all the problem related to this sequence has gone away. We now know that the urban beginnings including writing took place in the early Harappan phase itself, but still, between this phase and the Mature or classic phase of the Indus civilization, there is a great difference in scale. The problem now is to explain this change in scale – the explosion of activities in various spheres of life, which strongly contrast with the scale of what went on earlier in the same range of activities. In 1995 I tried to offer an explanation:

> Thus, it is postulated that within the framework of an ideology which cannot yet be defined in concrete social and institutional terms, an irrigation system, however simple, to cope with the problem of settling down in the riverine plains, and increased craft-specialization as seen by the presence of a large number of raw material types in the early Harappan level and the copper metallurgical area of the contemporary Ganeshwar culture, were two key variables in the emergence of the Indus civilization (Chakrabarti 1995/2001 reprint: 52).

Since 1995 there has been nothing in the archaeological record, which would need a revision of this opinion. The premise of an effective irrigation network in Sind in the Indus context has, in fact, been fully substantiated by the archival research on Sind's economic history in the late nineteenth and early twentieth centuries. The idea that the Indus agriculture depended on the annual over-bank flooding, like the case of the ancient Egypt where the Nile flooded the valley, has turned out to be completely wrong. Actually, the model is not that of Egypt but of Mesopotamia where the flow of the rivers was at a level higher than the level of the surrounding fields, and all that one had to do was to dig canals to take water to the fields. The Indus situation in Sind, as our ethnohistorical data show, has a strong ancient Mesopotamian parallel. As far as the intensification of craft activities is concerned, more data are being made available on the role of the Ganeshwar metallurgical area in the supply of both ores and implements to the Harappan belt of Haryana and Rajasthan.

Possehls's emphasis on the external trade to account for the "paroxysmal change that seems to have led to the development of the Indus civilization" runs counter to my thesis that it is not external trade but the other more internal factors like irrigation and intensification of craft activities which led to the transformation of the civilization from its early Harappan phase to the mature Harappan. In my detailed analysis of the Indus external trade I found it difficult "to suggest a causal link between the Indus external trade and the genesis of the Indus civilization" (Chakrabarti 1990: 169).

The sub-text of Possehl's trade-theory is that but for this trade with the outside world and the dissemination of ideas from there, the Indus civilization would not have emerged. This external trade is concomitant with the growth of the mature form of this civilization; this trade does not antedate it. Secondly, the quantum of this trade is certainly far less than the quantum of its internal trade – trade that looked after the distribution and exchange of the various types of raw materials from place to place in the vast network of the Indus civilization. Moreover, I do not think that the transformation from the early Harappan to the mature Harappan took place in a short time; there is no justification to describe this change as 'paroxysmal', as Possehl has done. For instance, assuming that the mature form of this civilization emerged around 2700/2600 BC, the writing itself began around 3300 BC, the date of the Ravi phase of Harappa. All that we can note here is that there is a great reluctance on the part of some archaeologists, of which Possehl is one, to agree with the notion that the origin of the Indus civilization is best understood exclusively in its own terms, i.e., in terms of the story of its own internal development.

4. Did the Indus civilization merge in the Historical Developmental Process of later India and form an Integral part of her Mainstream Cultural Development?

If one looks at the archaeological sequence of all the areas which were once covered by Indus civilization sites, one immediately realizes that, the decline of the civilization notwithstanding, there is no break in the archaeological sequence in any of the relevant areas, nor is there any evidence of new cultural inroads which cannot be explained geographically with reference to the Oxus-Indus-Pamir-eastern Iran political and economic interaction sphere. Further, in all these areas, the high tradition of the mature Indus civilization denotes a well-marked phase in the history of their very long cultural growth. For instance, in the Ghaggar-Hakra belt the sequence begins with Hakra ware, and at the newly excavated site of Bhirrana near Fatehabad this has been found to go back to the 5th millennium BC. On the other hand, the sequence of the area as a whole, moves through early, transitional and mature Harappa to the Painted Grey Ware, Northern Black Polished Ware and later historic levels.

I have personally done fieldwork only on the distribution of sites in western Uttar Pradesh between the Yamuna and the Shivalik foothills at the gate of Uttaranchal. This region has yielded a large number of sites which have been categorised as 'early', 'mature' and 'late' by many scholars including J.P. Joshi. Although some Harappan elements, including a seal and some script-signs incised on pottery, are present at some of these sites, it is doubtful if they can be given a specific place in the developmental sequence of the Harappan civilization. This feature has been worked out clearly at the site of Sinoli where many burials have recently been excavated. While Harappan artefacts like long barrel-cylinder carnelian seals and typical Harappan pottery forms have been found in the burial goods of this site, it contains typical upper Gangetic valley copper hoard implements like antennae-sword and its associated sheath. It was once argued (Chakrabarti and Lahiri 1996) that the copper hoards of the upper Gangetic valley belong to the late Harappan tradition, and the link between the Harappan tradition and these copper hoards has been verified at Sinoli. The Archaeological Survey of India website calls Sinoli a late Harappan site. However, that is doubtful. One has to wait for absolute dates from the site before ascribing any specific label to it. Our own hypothesis is that there was an early Harappan base in western UP, which served as the base of the Harappan tradition of this region. Sites like Sinoli (also written as Sanauli) near Baghpat developed in this context. The culture complex which was once identified as 'Bara' also seems to be linked to this context. More excavations and dates will be necessary before this context is properly understood.

One of its significant facts is that this tradition forms the base of the archaeological column which goes up to the historical periods in this vast region at the head of the Indo-Gangetic plain. One cannot get away from feeling that it was the Harappan tradition tempered with some still-to-be-identified regional elements, which laid down the roots of the entire cultural development of the upper Ganga plain. Among other things, how can we deny the significance of the antennae swords of the Gangetic valley copper hoards, which have now been verified to belong to the Harappan tradition?

This is a case which is unlikely to be true of only the upper Gangetic valley; looked at carefully, possibly all other Harappan distribution areas will be found to have well-marked regional elements, proving that the Harappan growth was not a monolithic growth. It may well be the case of different columns tied together by the element of its participation in varying proportions in the classic mature Harappan phenomenon which may in that context well signify the high Indian tradition of that period. That the people of this tradition were drifting towards the east and Gujarat in large numbers due to the accelerated drying-up of the Sarasvati during the late Harappan period between c. 2000 and c. 1400/1300 BC is very clear from the large concentrations of late Harappan sites in these regions.

It is largely from this point of view that I made the following comment in 2004:

> All the people of the subcontinent are, in one way or another, inheritors of the Indus civilization (Chakrabarti 2004: 22).

There are myriads of issues which drive us towards this assertion – the crafts which still survive, the pattern of both internal and external trade, the close familiarity with the regional topographies, sculpture, religion, and many more items besides. The high tradition of the Indian culture is certainly rooted in the Indus civilization. That its linkages had extended up to the deep south is shown not merely by the find of a polished celt with incised Harappan script signs from a place not far from Cuddalore on the eastern coast but by the find of a number of sites with antennae copper swords of the upper Gangetic valley copper hoard type as far as the Ramanathapuram district of Tamil Nadu and a tea estate in Kerala. The Harappan orbit, at a long remove, touched the deep south as well.

It is this which the crux of the socio-politics of the Indus civilization studies. There are scholars who do not simply like the idea of anything related to Hinduism in this civilization. I wrote in 2004:

> We do not suggest that Hinduism in its modern form was present in the Indus civilization, but some major elements of Hindu belief system seem to be present in the Indus finds (Chakrabarti 2004: 20).

This is an innocuous statement and there is nothing objectionable about it, but still there is a marked element of hostility towards such notions. There is also some literature seeking parallels for Indus art motifs and sculptural styles in Bactria and west Asia, although it is not easy to note any non-Indian tradition in the figure of *Sramana* from Mohenjodaro or any other sculptural relic of this civilization.

I have tried to argue that the interaction with the plough-based agriculturists of the Harappan tradition helped the transition of various incipient agriculturists of non-Harappan India to move towards effective agriculture as testified by the many agricultural areas of the third and second millennia BC (Chakrabarti 1995). This cannot be the only element in this transition, but it has to be counted as one of the major elements. This also partly explains the reason why the Harappan tradition lies at the root of development of the economic India of later periods.

4

The Sociopolitics of Some Debates in Early Historic Archaeology

There are three basic issues related to the initial stage of early historic Indian archaeology: the date of the early NBP and its spread outside the primary area; the dates of the beginning of writing and coinage; and the date of the Buddha. The third issue has been discussed in my *Colonial Indology: Sociopolitics of the Ancient Indian Past* in 1997 and does not concern us here. Here I shall be concerned only with the first two issues and their various ramifications.

I. THE LITERATURE ON THE NBP

The way the date of the NBP has been debated in Indian archaeology is most interesting. Even before A. Ghosh and K.C. Panigrahi wrote on this pottery in *Ancient India* no. 1 (1946) and called it Northern Black Polished Ware, this was a recognizable item both on the surface and in the excavations of the major city sites. Among others, Alexander Cunningham was aware of this pottery, and as early as 1915, Marshall dated it at Bhita in the eighth century BC, mainly on the basis of the neatly laid down floor-levels of the site.

The publication which has controlled Indian mind for many years regarding the NBP is Mortimer Wheeler's *Early India and Pakistan to Ashoka* (1959). He made a number of points: (1) it first appears in northern India shortly after forged iron; (2) it may also be linked to the "liking of the Persians for a high metallic polish, as represented very notably in some of their masonry; (3) on the basis of the depth at which it occurs below surface at the Bhir and Sirkap mounds of the ancient city of *Takshasila*, it was ascribed to the fifth-second centuries BC, with the possibility of its continuation in still later contexts.

> ... even at Taxila itself, its arrival should mostly be equated with the spread of the Mauryan domination from the Ganges to these parts after 323 BC. In other words, I would provisionally ascribe the NBP Ware of the north-westerly regions of the subcontinent to the period 320-150 BC, without prejudice to the possibility of an appreciably earlier beginning in the Ganges Basin itself (Wheeler 1959: 31).

This dating was done before the radiocarbon dating of the NBP-bearing sites was available. However, even after the appearance of this method of dating in the scene, this date-bracket was not disputed by all. For instance, in what seems to be an editorial note to T.N. Roy's article on the NBP and associated wares in the first volume of *An Encyclopaedia of Indian Archaeology* (ed. A. Ghosh, 1989), the following opinion has been given:

> On the whole, however, calibration of C-14 dates apart, the dates originally proposed by Wheeler and Krishna Deva, 1946, p. 56, viz., the 5th to the early part of the 2nd century, can still be regarded as holding the ground with marginal adjustments (Ghosh 1989, Vol. 1, p. 256)

Roy's own opinion was that the evidence could loosely confine this pottery to a period from 600 BC to 100 BC (Ghosh 1989: 255).

Outside the Gangetic plain, especially in Central India, the Deccan and the south, the appearance of the NBP is usually thought to be considerably later than its Ganga plain occurrence. For instance, at Kaundinyapur to the west of Nagpur, this phase is supposed to belong only to 300 BC (Ghosh 1989: 211). Examples like this are many and have been conditioned by the belief that the NBP spread mainly along the axis of Mauryan dynastic expansion. This ignores the fact that the linkages between the Ganga plain and the Deccan are very close and marked by well-defined routes along which trade and cultural elements must have disseminated more rapidly than we are willing to admit. In retrospect, one is also surprised by the fact that Marshall's early dating of the NBP at Bhita was not even considered worthy of discussion in the *Ancient India* article on the NBP.

Assuming that the NBP in the local archaeological sequence denotes the beginning of early historic period, the lower dating of the NBP outside the Gangetic plain has, to a great extent, distorted our perception of the date of the beginning of the early historic period in those areas. For instance, the earliest date of the NBP at Dharanikota or Amaravati in Andhra is about 500 calibrated BC, and on this basis alone, the beginning of the early historic period in Andhra can be placed firmly around 500 BC. This is also the calibrated date of the NBP at the site of Wari Bateshwar in the Meghna delta of Bangladesh. At Alagankulam at the mouth of the Vaigai near Madura, the NBP occurs in a stratigraphic context on which specific stratigraphic information is not available. However, this NBP material is preserved in the Tamil Nadu State archaeology department office in Chennai, and having examined the material the Director of Uttar Pradesh State archaeology department opined that the material was identical with the early NBP from various sites in Uttar Pradesh. At Korkai, a little to the south of Alagankulam, there is a lone date from an NBP-associated level in the region of about 900 calibrated BC. In the NBP core area, i.e., the central Ganga plain, there is a consistent series of dates putting the emergence of this pottery in the eighth-seventh century BC, if not somewhat earlier. One does not think that its emergence in other areas has to be deemed considerably later.

Although the presence of the NBP in the archaeological sequences of other areas indicates in a way the existence of early historic phase in those areas, the regional pottery correlates of the early historic period outside the Ganga plain still remain to be worked out in detail. For instance, according to K. Rajan (personal discussion) russet-coated ware is the index pottery of the early historic pottery in the Coimbatore area of Tamil Nadu whereas in the southernmost part of the same province and in Sri Lanka the black-and-red ware with occasional white paintings is supposedly the distinguishing ceramic feature of this period. Moreover, the date of the first appearance of the NBP in different regions has to be independently established. The belief that it was comparatively late outside the central Ganga plain may be wrong because there is no reason why the NBP could not disseminate rapidly outside its core area along the trade routes of the day (Chakrabarti 2006: 311).

The preceding passage should not give the impression that the date of the NBP has been satisfactorily settled in all areas. For instance, according to S.K. Jha (1998: 258- 263) the premise which has hitherto been generally accepted that the NBP originated in the middle Ganga plain sites like Rajgir, Pataliputra, Champa, etc. cannot be considered valid in the light of the growing radiocarbon dating evidence which puts primary emphasis on the central Ganga plain, especially the portion in Uttar Pradesh. As he writes,

(i) The middle Gangetic plains, especially Bihar, cannot be considered as the place of origin of the NBP.

(ii) It did not have a spatial movement from east to west. If it was other way round, that also cannot be established undisputedly. But then, at the present stage of our knowledge, it appears to be more acceptable than the former course of movement (Jha 1998: 263).

Since Marshall commented on the probable date of the NBP at Bhita being c. 800 BC, the chronological study of this diagnostic early historic pottery of the Ganga plain has come a full circle. It has been re-instated at 800 BC, with the possibility of its being even somewhat earlier, if the unpublished dates from Ayodhya are any indication. There never was any cogent reason to bring it down to the fifth century BC, nor was there any ground to associate with the Mauryan expansion. In view of the extensive trade network of protohistoric and early historic India, the distribution of a particular type of pottery in various areas need not carry any other implication than the fact that the concerned areas were interlinked by trade and travel. To say that the find of the NBP outside its primary area, i.e., the Ganga valley, was due to the expansion of Buddhism or Mauryan power cannot be called cases of good historical generalizations. The fact that the study of the distribution of the NBP had to remain long in the shadow of Wheeler's analysis in 1959 is a good enough indication of the study of early historic Indian archaeology being chained to publications by important people without subjecting them to close scrutiny.

II. THE BEGINNING OF WRITING

This tendency has been equally marked in the case of determining the chronology of the beginning of writing and coinage in India, especially writing. The archaeological datum-line is the reign of

Asoka (272-232 BC) when there were royal edicts of various kinds in various parts of his empire from south Afghanistan to Karnataka. These edicts are standardised declarations of royal injunctions and expressed in scripts which would be known to the people for whom they were intended. Scholars have also detected in them some regional variations of language and script. By any reckoning, these edicts written in Brahmi, Kharosthi (only in the North Western Frontier), Greek (south Afghanistan) and Aramaic (south Afghanistan and Punjab) suggest wide knowledge of writing even among the common people and a fairly long history of evolution of these scripts. This is exactly what has been denied by many epigraphists including such scholars as D.C. Sircar and A.H. Dani. No cogent argument has been given by these scholars anywhere; it is only their assumption or, if one prefers, *ex cathedra* statement.

There was a time when a few inscriptions including the famous Sohgaura copper-plate inscription used to be considered pre-Mauryan. One also remembers K.P. Jayaswal's reading of the inscriptions on Patna Yakshas which he ascribed palaeographically to the pre-Asokan phase. Currently, of course, scholars pointblank refuse to accept the possibility that some of the early written material which has come down to us could date from before the phase of the Asokan edicts. One does not really know how and why this has come about.

I think that the main reason is the unwillingness to consider the facts that India has had a long tradition of writing on birch-bark and palm leaves using various kinds of bone and metallic stylus and that the tradition of pre-Asokan writing consisted precisely of this. This has not survived, just as the material written on the perishable materials in the Indus civilization has not survived. Because of its very character, i.e., the perishableness of the material on which it was written, even the existence of such material is only assumption. However, as everybody knows, the tradition of such writing continued at the grassroots level well into the nineteenth century, and in the literature of that period one reads of people sitting in their courtyards and preparing accounts on palm leaves with the help of iron stylus. In the ancient context, there are enough epigraphic references to the fact that the records of the day-to-day administration were maintained in written documents made of perishable materials. The presence of dynastic archives and chronicles has also been attested to in inscriptions.

Scholars like Rajabali Pandey and Gouri Shankar Ojha compiled an impressive mass of literary material to argue that there was enough evidence to suggest the beginning of early historic writing in India as early as the seventh/eighth century BC. The data, of course, are disjointed, like any other corpus of literary data in the context of early India, but the general trend of evidence is indisputable. One can, of course, pick up this literary evidence piece by piece and try to demonstrate that none of them has a cast-iron basis. To be honest, this is exactly the way in which the Puranic evidence of the dynastic succession in Magadha was torn down while arguing a late date for the life of the Buddha. However, we cannot simply push away the bits of evidence which do not suit our premise, because in many cases the general fabric of the study of ancient Indian history depends on the frame built by such bits of evidence.

As far as the evidence of the beginning of early historic writing is concerned, it possibly needs a special frame of mind to argue that Panini wrote his famous grammar of Sanskrit in the fifth/fourth century BC when the writing had not yet been invented in India or that the extensive *Jataka* evidence to writing is not dependable because chronologically this evidence is not cast-iron. In the case of the *Jatakas* it is conveniently forgotten that they were composed in a period when Varanasi was an independent kingdom and that it lost its sovereignty to Magadha in the sixth century BC. I have also pointed out the significance of the occurrence of *Bhurjapatra* or birch-bark in Period II (tenth to seventh century BC) of Sringaverapura. The precise chronological point of this occurrence cannot be determined, but considering that birch-bark was a well-known material to write on, in ancient India, it is reasonable to infer that this material was being transported about 500 km from the hills of central Garhwal precisely because the southern fringe of the upper Gangetic valley was familiar with writing by that time.

The point which I find inexplicable is the general scholarly refusal even to admit the implication of the fact that there seems to be enough circumstantial evidence to point out an earlier beginning of writing in India than the third century BC reign of Asoka.

Nowhere has this refusal more sordid than in the case of determining the beginning of early history in Tamil Nadu and the date of early Tamil-Brahmi inscriptions of that region.

There is not a shadow of doubt that the Sri Lankan ancient city site of Anuradhapura has potsherds incised with Tamil-Brahmi around the middle of the first millennium BC, apparently by the seventh-eighth century BC. The implication of this date on the date of occurrence of similar incised sherds and rock inscriptions in various parts of Tamil Nadu is enormous, suggesting a similar early date for at least some of the material. Although the Anuradhapura discovery is now more than a decade old, there seems to be a steadfast refusal on the part of Indian epigraphers even to consider the possibility of the beginning of writing in Tamil Nadu earlier than the magic datum-line of third century BC. For instance, a Tamil epigrapher as renowned as I. Mahadevan is apparently unwilling to consider this possibility, and well-known archaeologists like K.S. Ramachandran quite determinedly ignore any C-14 date from Tamil Nadu, which may be used as an evidence to argue for an early beginning of the historical period in that region.

The way in which the significance of the four available radiocarbon dates from Period II of Alagunkalam at the mouth of the Vaigai river has been ignored is perhaps surprising. All these uncalibrated dates – 380 +/- 105 BC, 355+/- 135 BC, 255+/- 105 BC and 205 +/-105 BC – belong to Period II at the site and give a clear sweep in the second-half of the first millennium BC. A span of 400-100 BC can only be a conservative chronological estimate for Alagankulam, Period II. This period here yields red ware, black-and-red ware, rouletted ware, mat-design pottery, grey ware, inscribed sherds, stamped sherds and amphorae sherds, the dominant pottery being the rouletted ware. The excavators' estimate of chronology for this period is 300 BC-100 BC, but apparently, this ignores the element of calibration.

Period I of Alagunkalam has red ware, black-and-red ware, mat-design pottery, NBP and grey ware and its dominant pottery is black-and-red ware. There is no radiocarbon date from this level, and the excavators' chronology puts it between 500 BC and 300 BC. I think that there is enough justification to put it between the bracket 700/800 BC to 400 BC. The NBP occurs in the upper level and may be put anywhere between 500 and 400 BC.

There is little doubt that by 500/400 BC Alagankulam gets drawn into the historical orbit of the Ganga plain. The local beginning of the early historic context should be earlier, although it cannot be precisely defined yet. A tentative date of 500 BC seems to be eminently acceptable.

Natana Kasinathan, a former archaeologist Director of Tamil Nadu State Department of Archaeology, has analysed the chronological implication of the find of inscribed potsherds at the site in Period II. The inscribed potsherds occur in layers 2 to 5, and the layer 5 bears a punch-marked coin.

The punch-marked coin found in the layer 5 of AGM-10 is believed to have been issued by the Nanda kingdom and was in circulation from fourth century BC, according to Thiru R. Krishnamurthy, the eminent numismatist of Tamil Nadu (Sridhar 2005: 92).

Pointing out that this level could belong to the fourth century BC itself, Kasinathan argues that "the inscribed sherds of these layers would be the sheet anchor for dating the inscriptions on potteries and also the rock bed inscriptions of future discoveries" (Sridhar 2005: 93). The following comment by Kasinathan is worth quoting because this highlights his idea of a relationship between the sherds inscribed with Tamil-Brahmi script:

> While discussing about the archaic Tamil inscriptions, it is imperative to deal with the graffiti-bearing potsherds also. In all the historical places the inscribed potsherds occur either in the same level of the graffiti-bearing sherds or in the overlying level of it. Hence the study of graffiti sherds may pave the way to solve the dating problem of archaic Tamil inscriptions (Sridhar 2005: 94).

More evidence on the beginning of writing in Tamil Nadu comes from Kodumanal near Coimbatore and Vallam near Tanjore.

The Kodumanal evidence has been clearly discussed by its excavator K. Rajan who puts it the beginning of Kodumanal Period I at least in the fifth century BC. The relationship between the graffiti on the local black-and-red ware is noteworthy: some of the graffiti marks are found incised at the end of the Brahmi inscriptions on the same sherds, and Rajan's close study of their symbols, places of occurrence, frequency and position demonstrates that "they were used to convey a certain message either pictographically or ideographically". The same relationship has been observed at places like Vallam and Mangudi (near Madurai). In Period I, phase 1 of Vallum there are only graffiti and no Brahmi script. In the phase 2 of the same period, there are both graffiti and Brahmi script, and in its phase 3 there is only Brahmi script.

The entire evidence is remarkably striking as far as the regional base of the Tamil-Brahmi script is concerned. The fact that the earliest level of Vallum belongs to the end of the second millennium BC (calibrated) makes it an interesting site, showing the early base of the graffiti tradition in south India (for the Tamil Nadu situation, Chakrabarti 2006).

Considering all these factors into consideration, it is virtually impossible in the current context to deny that the beginning of early history in the Kaveri delta and the adjoining region did not take place around 500 BC. The question is why some scholars have not yet woken up to this fact. The answer can only be tentative and even strictly circumstantial. There is a body of Tamil scholars who are generally Brahmins and feel that the Dravidian belt emerged into civilization only due to contact with the Aryans from the north. Bergunder (2004) has commented in detail on some of them.

For instance, he cites Srinivasa Aiyangar who wrote in 1914 that before the Brahmins migrated to south India 'there was no literature worth the name among the Tamils'. This was the general Brahmanical view of south Indian history, of which an idea can also be had from the writings of such scholars as Swaminatha Aiyar and Krishnaswami Aiyangar, both of whom wrote in the 1920s. According to Aiyar, as cited by Bergunder (2004: 77-78) the Dravidian civilization "is really the civilization of the Aryans and Aryanized immigrants from the North" and there is "no reason to suppose that the Dravidian languages were once spoken throughout India". According to Krishnaswami Aiyangar (Bergunder 2004: 78), the history of India begins with the coming of the Aryans and similarly, the history of south India too "begins with the coming of the Aryans into the South".

I cannot judge if this is still the general attitude – conscious or unconscious – of the south Indian Bramanical community towards the history of this region, but when I find two highly respected Tamil Brahmin scholars like I. Mahadevan and K.S. Ramachandran virtually refusing to consider the possibility of a pre-third century BC beginning for the historic period in Tamil Nadu, I cannot help pondering over the Brahmanical view of south Indian history, of which this seems to be a good example.

III. THE ROLE OF IRON IN THE SECOND URBANISATION

The controversy is somewhat dated, but as the volume *Iron and Social Change in Early India* edited by Bhairavi Prasad Sahu (2004) shows, it still enjoys some relevance in the field of ancient Indian historical studies. As far as I can judge, the idea is rooted in V. Gordon Childe's Huxley Memorial lecture for 1944: 'archaeological ages as technological stages' (Childe 1944). In this article Childe postulated two 'modes' of the use of iron. In the first 'mode' iron tools were often slavish copies of the stone or bronze tools, whereas new species and even new genera of iron tools emerged in the second 'mode'. Regarding the Iron Age he commented:

> During the Iron Age a new type of civilization was first firmly established. I should not dream of contending that iron if itself evoked the *polis*. I am prepared to argue that the Mediterranean city state was impossible without the transport facilities iron tools could alone provide (Childe 1944: 23).

The influence of the above comments made by Childe on the Iron Age exerted a lot of influence on the writings of Indian Marxists on the understanding of early historic India. Here one may note in background that Gordon Childe's writings were very popular in the Indian communist circles in the 1950s and later. Childe was a friend of one of the leading members of the early communist movement in Britain, Rajani Palme Dutt who had also a great influence on the beginning of the communist movement in India. Childe's books were recommended reading in the communist study-circles in Bengal in the 1960s.

The term 'second urbanisation' was used, as far as one knows, first by H.D. Sankalia in the volume edited by R.J. Braidwood and G.R. Wiley, *Courses toward Urban Life* (Braidwood and Wiley 1962) to denote the phase of the growth of early historic cities in India, especially in the Ganga valley. That iron had a close link with its development possibly found its first clear expression in D.D. Kosambi's books *An Introduction to the Study of Ancient Indian History* (Kosambi 1956) and *The Culture and Civilization of Ancient India in Historical Outline* (Kosambi 1965) where it was argued that without the effective use of iron tools the deep forests of the Ganga plain could not be cleared, and thus there was a direct link between the technological impact of the use of iron and the growth of Gangetic cities. R.S. Sharma imbibed Childe's notion of technological 'modes', tried to apply them to the Indian Iron Age context and strongly underlined the significance of iron use in his *Material Culture and Social Formation in Ancient India* (Sharma 1983), among his other publications.

However, Sharma's treatment of the problem suffers from some serious misunderstanding of the archaeological evidence. In the 2001 reprint of this book he begins by categorically asserting that the later Vedic period "coincides with the first phase of the use of iron in northern India" (Sharma 1983-2001 reprint: 71), thus clearly identifying the Painted Grey Ware phase of the upper Ganga plain and the Indo-Gangetic divide with the later Vedic period. It seems that the only basis of his doing so is the apparent similarity between Max Muller's chronology of the later Vedic period and the date of the Painted Grey Ware in the first-half of the first millennium BC. Equally, if not more, unacceptable is his following statement:

> But so far very few iron tools belonging to the first-half of the first millennium have been discovered, which suggests that at this stage iron did not contribute to handicrafts and agriculture. Most iron artefacts from the PGW levels comprise arrowheads and spearheads supplemented by nails. At Jakhera in Eta district in UP a ploughshare has also been discovered, but this might belong to c. 500 BC (Sharma 1983/2001 reprint: 72).

According to Sharma, northern India did not enter Iron Age till the sixth century BC and there were more agricultural implements only in the NBP period between 500 and 200 BC (his date of the NBP period).

> In the first phase in India, the use of iron could not be extended to production because of its paucity and primitive technology, but it may have helped the organizers of production in making their authority felt over the producers. However, in this phase iron may have been used for clearance, for making wheels and the body of carts and chariots, and in the construction of houses because nails have been recovered from several PGW sites (Sharma 1983/2001 reprint: 72).

It is obvious that the accuracy of archaeological facts is irrelevant to Sharma's line of argument. Iron begins in northern India not in the PGW phase but in the earlier Black-and-Red Ware phase which at Malhar goes back to c. 1800 BC and at Dadupur to around the middle of the second millennium BC. We have already mentioned the occurrence of an iron ploughshare at Malhar as early as the first occurrence of iron at the site. To argue that there were agricultural implements of iron in northern India only in the NBP phase is to completely ignore the relevant archaeological situation. Vibha Tripathi's division of the Indian Iron Age into Early Iron Age and Middle Iron Age (Tripathi 2001) does not seem to carry much archaeological weight because she puts sites from different areas in each of these stages, and that really cannot be said to have much meaning. For instance, what does one gain by putting Atranjikhera, Chirand, Naikund and Hallur all together in the Early Iron Age bracket?

Some Indian archaeologists took to Kosambi's idea of the importance of iron technology in the Gangetic plain with enthusiasm:

> With the advent of iron into the doab, jungles were cleared, swamps were drained and agriculture flourished. Agricultural surplus gave rise to cities and urban life (Agrawal 1982: 263)

Not all archaeologists were however willing to toe the line of D.P. Agrawal and the Marxist scholars from whom he got his idea. This too has a long intellectual background. By the 1960s the archaeological opinion was divided between Childe's technological determinism and the importance of social-institutional changes propounded by scholars like Braidwood, R.M. Adams and others in the background of Childe's 'Urban Revolution'. A brief examination of the problem in the Indian context was made by the present author in 1972-73 under the rubric of 'concept of the Urban Revolution and the Indian context' (Chakrabarti 1972-73). The present author argued that the Indian data supported the primacy of social-institutional model. In 1973 A. Ghosh (1973) characterized the impact of the early use of iron in India as slow and something limited in its impact, an opinion which was also echoed by the present author in 1974 (Chakrabarti 1973; for further development of the idea, Chakrabarti and Lahiri 1994). The notion that iron tools played a leading role in creating a social surplus in the Iron Age of the Ganga plain was disputed by Makkhan Lal in 1986 (Lal 1986).

All these early studies have been largely superseded by Rakesh Tewari's recent study of the problem (Tewari 2004) and also by his discoveries of early iron in the central Ganga plain dating from c. 1800 BC.

> On the basis of literary, palynological and archaeological evidence discussed in this paper, the following conclusions may be proposed. The long-standing view regarding the prevalence of dense forests over the entire Ganga plain to the east of the Yamuna and their clearance after the mass production of iron artefacts for large-scale human occupation is not tenable. Palynological and botanical studies carried out in the upper Ganga plain are indicative of a savannah landscape dominated by grassy vegetation along with thicker wooded pockets from about 15000 yr BP ... Sufficient open land was available along rivers and lakes, both in the upper Ganga plain and the middle Ganga plain, to accommodate human settlements and required agricultural fields. A considerable number of such settlement sites datable between circa 2500 and 800 BC have already been recorded from these areas. Advanced agriculture was in practice in the upper and middle Ganga plains well before the introduction of iron (Tewari 2004: 113).

Tewari's own work at Malhar and Dadupur show that between 1800 and 1500 BC the use of iron was extensive in the central Ganga plain – extensive enough to include an iron plough in the Malhar artefact inventory. There was certainly a trade network of iron linking different parts of the central Ganga plain during this period, and when one considers that early historic urban growth in the region cannot be taken before c. 800 BC here, one realizes that the impact of iron on the Gangetic economy could not have been fast and revolutionary in its scope, however much the Indian Marxists with their unshakeable faith in Gordon Childe's theories try to establish a causal link between iron and early historic Indian urbanisation.

5

Summary and Discussion

The 'endnotes' of our introduction are meant to give an idea of the heat which has been generated recently over the Sarasvati project, Aryan invasion theory, Indian and Californian textbook controversy, the setting up of an academic body to study Vedic culture, etc. Behind the heat and dust of such battles, however, there is a steady academic pattern, and it is this pattern which has led to these battles in the first place. The main purpose of this book was to briefly explore this pattern in the context of Indian archaeology. What has emerged, even after a brief analysis as ours, is a scenario which should set us thinking about the future of historical studies, of which archaeological studies are a part, in modern India.

In the introductory essay I have laid some emphasis on my own point of view, i.e., the archaeology of the subcontinent should primarily be viewed in its own terms unless there is a clear and verifiable evidence to the contrary. The subcontinent, like any other area of the world, has always interacted with the areas beyond its borders and its history and culture have certainly been enriched in various ways through this interaction. This is not in dispute, but what is in dispute is the extent to which we have to view the entire developmental pattern of the subcontinent in the light of what came from outside, ignoring the possibilities of any originality or innovation in the land itself. It is not merely an issue of 'migration versus indigenism'; it is much more than that. It is also a question of what we seek to learn about our ancient history. Do we focus on what was happening in the land itself, using all the tools of modern research, or do we remain content with the framework of the past that we have historically received and is rooted in the nebulous world of 'race' and 'comparative philology'? The latter approach was given the rubric 'colonial Indology' by me (Chakrabarti 1997). There is, in fact, no room for choice. If the study of ancient India has to move forward, with emphasis on peoples' history and not on mushy and undefined 'wonder that was India', we have no other option but to discard the 'colonial' approach and relate our history to the land. It is unfortunate that this 'paradigm shift' has not yet occurred in the context of ancient Indian historical studies, even sixty years after Independence. Remaining shackled to any particular model – colonial or otherwise – is not an enervating thing for any discipline. The fact that the Indian archaeological studies are still almost totally under the shadow of the old colonial frame of perception is a tragedy in the history of the discipline, if not in the history of the nation.

To be honest, Indian archaeology is unlikely to be alone in retaining this feature. The issues of migration, race, etc. have not gone away even from the mainstream Euro-American archaeology. They have only relocated their space in the archaeological scheme under the new rubrics of 'ethnicity', 'historical linguistics' and/or archaeo-genetics. Tracing language history and dispersal through archaeo-genetics which is dependent on DNA studies is considered a very much innovative idea, and these days, the problem of agricultural origins in many parts of the world, especially southeast Asia, is tied to the determination of the language of the early agriculturists. Grand modern schemes of historical linguistics are explained and inferences made about their possible corollaries in the domain of archaeological cultures. Two simple points, however, get ignored in such undertakings. First, are these particularly relevant historical questions? When there is no known literature in a specific archaeological or historical context, what does one gain by speculating on the probable identity of the language which was spoken by the concerned people? Further, is the methodology of determining such languages clearly defined? Are the premises and chronologies of historical linguistics testable, and has it been explained why the premises of modern 'historical linguists' are more dependable or 'scientific' than those of the eighteenth-twentieth century 'comparative philology'? Attempts at historical reconstruction on the basis of the so-called 'linguistic palaeontology' have been well-known since the nineteenth century. In India, for instance, N.R. Banerjee, as late as

1965, devoted a lot of space in his book on the Indian Iron Age to explain it in the light of what he described as 'linguistic palaeontology'(Banerjee 1965). Did it lead anywhere except a historical reconstruction based on a turgid mixture of biology, language and culture, precisely the sort of mix one should perhaps avoid in modern historical and archaeological studies. The old mixture led to outrageous diffusionary reconstructions of human history; are modern archaeologists ready to accept such reconstructions? In some areas of the world, there is apparently no problem. For instance, in his analysis of "Asian farming diasporas? agriculture, languages, and genes in China and southeast Asia", Peter Bellwood, a noted protagonist of this kind of approach, assumes that the early forms of major language families in this vast region – Sino-Tibetan, Austroasiatic, Hmong-Mien, Austronesian and Tai – "were at one time located sufficiently close together for some degree of sharing of heritage, both generic and areal". This he relates to the expansion of rice and millet cultivation from central China to southeast Asia and the Pacific, further suggesting that "early agricultural economies, and foundation languages at the bases of language families, spread hand in hand". One of the problems is that he does not explain the extent to which his reconstruction of the language families concerned and his premise of the moving out of these families towards southeast Asia and the Pacific along with the spread of rice and millet cultivation differ from the nineteenth century premise of the Austro-Asiatic language family being the representatives of early agriculturists at least in southeast Asia and eastern India. It is also apparent that he does not admit of the possibility of multiple independent beginnings of rice cultivation, whereas it is precisely the possibility of such beginnings in the case of rice which has been indicated by some recent research: "the combined genetic and geographic data provide strong evidence for multiple domestications of cultivated rice"(Londo *et al.* 2006). More interestingly, professional experts have commented on J. Diamond and P. Bellwood's 2003 article in *Science*, "Farmers and their languages: the first expansions" where they comment that further progress will depend on research based on a combination of archaeology, crop and livestock studies, physical anthropology, genetics and linguistics (Diamond and Bellwood 2003). That the inquiries along all these lines of investigation will result in a consensus of views is something which can be ignored straightaway. In their comments on this article by Diamond and Bellwood this is what Victor Golla *et al.* (2003) say:

> One of their "clearest examples" from the Eastern Hemisphere, the spread of Austronesian languages, muddles the record by spuriously linking disparate cultural-history events.

Steven Oppenheimer (2004) has been equally forthright. He says that the Austronesian language/rice-farming equation suffers from certain methodological errors which include over-reliance on a 'controversial putative linguistic homeland' and "failure to deal with parallel evidence impartially". The problem also lies in ignoring the fact that the multiple lines of evidence "requires its own dating method if self-fulfilling assertions and circularity are to be avoided" (also, Oppenheimer 2006).

One does not also know that the type of evidence which archaeo-genetics offers for population movements is invariably consistent or not. In India, for instance, we have already noted how a previous DNA study made by a paedetrician from Utah, USA found that the upper caste Indians "are significantly more similar to Europeans than are the lower castes", whereas a more recent study points towards "a largely South Asian origin for Indian caste communities and therefore argue against any major influx, from regions north and west of India, of people associated either with the development of agriculture or the spread of the Indo-Aryan language family"(Sahoo *et al.* 2006).

If the claims of biology-language-culture mix are both unreliable and redolent of nineteenth century diffusionism of the German *Kulturekries* school, no less unacceptable is the modern archaeological quest to trace ethnicity in the archaeological record. Ethnic terms certainly occur in ancient literature, but the nature of ethnicity is ever-changing, and to try to trace this record in pre/non-literate archaeology is not perhaps a highly edifying exercise. The problem gets more confounded when one asks why there should be so much interest in chasing a nebulous category which may have some importance in the modern multicultural situations but is possibly entirely untraceable materially in the past.

Two other points need perhaps highlighting in our 'introduction': the theme of 'colonization' which runs through the writings of some of our important scholars, and a frankly perplexing obsession with the Aryans and Aryan Invasion Theory, only a small portion of which has been outlined in one of the endnotes of our 'introduction'. On one level, the emphasis on the colonization theme is nothing but the concerned scholars' inability to go beyond the ruling neo-colonial paradigm of the day. Similarly, Elizabeth Rosen Stone's view that the development of Indian art was influenced in various subtle ways by the artistic tradition in the lands to the west may be reminiscent of Vincent Smith's perception of Indian art, but this only brings out the attitude of the western art historical scholarship to India. This is an entirely colonial attitude, although in some recent publications there are some attempts to tone it down, without denying it altogether.

The intensity of the recent literature on the Aryans is somewhat inexplicable. Most of it is from outside the professional Indological circuit, but that is no cause for worry, particularly because the literature concerned is marked by both careful assessment of the relevant publications and critical acumen. The professional scholars have been immersed in their cocoons of vested interest for long, and it is indeed great that the criticism has emerged from plain-speaking enthusiasts who do not have to play by the rules laid down for them by the academic warlords of various kinds. The only jarring element that I personally find in this literature is the details with which even plainly nebulous opinions have been cited and refuted! On the other hand, the determination of some ruling academics of the day to throttle the dissenting voice is distressingly unpalatable. To relegate it unceremoniously to the camp of Hindu fundamentalism has neither logic nor decency behind it (for a recent attempt of this kind by a Western Indologist with a Ph.D in Sanskrit, Fosse 2005). In the Western universities interest in Sanskrit derives from the general and widespread interest in Indo-European linguistics. It is doubtful if it has much to do with anything else except grammar and sundry linguistic matters. One is not sure if the Sanskrit undergraduates in the Western campuses are even introduced to the beauty of Sanskrit poetical and dramatic literature. One cannot really regret the stoppage of the teaching of Sanskrit in the undergraduate frame of studies in such campuses, however long Sanskrit may have been taught in some of these places. So, one is not surprised that Sanskritists, especially Western Sanskritists, would be very upset by the very thought of dismantling the Indo-European/Aryan structure.

From my point of view, what is regrettable is that even the dissenting literature does not propose to do away with the category of Aryans altogether; in fact, in this area, I find their attitude somewhat ambivalent. B.B. Lal forcefully argues that the Rigveda could have been composed only in the subcontinental soil, and this is something with which only a rabid Aryanist with dreams of great Aryan migrations will find fault. What is somewhat saddening is that in this debate people have not hesitated even to distort, possibly wilfully, the meanings of texts, as Lal points out.

I have already drawn attention to P.V. Kane's dating of the Rigveda to the 6th millennium BC and later on the basis of what he considers to be unimpeachable astronomical calculations. It is interesting to reflect that this is also what S.S. Misra has argued recently, although on a different line of thought. His thinking is that "Sanskrit deserves a highly archaic status and on the basis of the archaic linguistic structure a much earlier date than the date given by European scholars" (Misra 2005: 224). He takes it back to c. 5000 BC by pointing out that the earliest loan-words in the Uralic languages are Rigvedic and that 5000 BC was the date of the earliest such loan-words in the opinion of J. Harmatta. It is not possible for me to comment on such 'linguistic datings' but one would think that it was virtually impossible to date linguistic changes or loan-words and that the method of 'glottochronology' by which one could chronologically pinpoint the history of language separations has not by and large satisfactorily worked. So, this part of Misra's argument is entirely speculative, and its importance from our point of view lies in the fact that this was the opinion of a man who has published on Indo-European linguistics.

The astronomical basis of the dating of the Vedic literature has recently received consideration from S.C. Kak as well (Kak 2006). He divides this literature into three phases: the early Vedic period (6000? – 4000 BC); the Rigvedic period (4000-2000 BC) and the phase of Brahmanical astronomy (2000-1000 BC). One is not sure if the literature would permit such a neat chronological phasing, especially when the date of the Brahmanical phase is derived from a purely speculative date of the drying of the Sarasvati. What it shows, however, is that the astronomical events mentioned in this literature can lead to a wide range of dates, which is not at all surprising in view of the breadth of the Vedic literature.

The professional archaeological attitude, apart from that of B.B. Lal, has not emerged from this issue with flying colours. In 1997, in his book on Indian protohistory M.K. Dhavalikar could not resist the temptation of adding a chapter on "archaeology of the Aryans" where the horse-bones of Harappan sites are relegated only to the late Harappan levels and the existence of spoked wheels in this civilization is admitted.

> The only evidence available is that in the second millennium BC, the Late Harappans had occupied the land of Sapta-Sindhu. They lived in small villages, built mud huts with thatched roofs, and their mixed economy was based on subsistence agriculture, stock-raising and hunting-fishing. The culture of the Aryans as reflected in the Rigveda was not much different. The circumstantial evidence thus would suggest that the Late Harappans may actually be the Rigvedic Aryans (Dhavalikar 1997: 300).

In 2006 J.M. Kenoyer seeks his Aryans in the late Harappan milieu too (Kenoyer 2006). It is apparently one thing to say that there is no archaeological evidence of Aryan migration to India, and it is quite another to deny the very notion of Aryans or Aryan migration. Kenoyer writes:

> The complex process of change after the Harappan period begins with the Late Harappan to Painted Grey Ware transition (1900-800 BCE) .... It is during this transition that we see the emergence of Vedic cultural traditions, characterized by a distinct ideology and language (Kenoyer 2006: 34-35).

In another publication dated in the same year Kenoyer (2006a) discusses the details of the Cemetery H level excavated by the American archaeological group at Harappa and jumps to conclusion that this reflects "social, economic and ideological restructuring that involved previously marginal or minority communities". The anthropological profundity of this conclusion is not clear to the present author, but he goes on to add: "The origin of these communities is unknown, but it is not unlikely that one or more of them may represent communities referred to in the early Vedic literature" (Kenoyer 2006a). If there is an iota of logic in this argument, I regret that I have been unable to find it.

Dhavalikar and Kenoyer are, of course, happy with the Rigvedic chronology they have got from Max Muller and scholars of that school. They do not share the anxiety of Winternitz and numerous others about the reality of the Rigvedic date being vastly different. They are quite happy with the dominant frame of thought and remain content only by pointing out the archaeological phase when, according to them, the Aryans could be accommodated.

It is interesting that the Californian textbook controversy should be so dominated by the notion of Aryan invasion of India. The vehemence with which this notion was defended is a commentary on the strength of the orthodox frame of ancient Indian studies both in and out of India. No quarter was asked for and none given! It is certainly one of the most bizarre academic debates anywhere but serves the purpose of showing that when the ruling paradigms of history are questioned, they do not fade in silence but put up a most stubborn resistance.

The Aryan theory has never been a purely academic or linguistic reconstruct. If my review of the Aryan theory (Chakrabarti 1997) in the Indian context has revealed anything, it is that it has been tinged with blatant racism throughout. That this racial tinge is not yet over can easily be shown by citing two authors, one Indian and the other an American. Writing on the Aryans in his *Ancient India in Historical Outline* D.N. Jha, a former General President of the Indian History Congress, comments,

> It is likely that the early Aryans had some consciousness of their distinctive physical appearance. They were generally fair, the indigenous people dark in complexion. The colour of the skin may have been an important mark of their identity (Jha 1998: 49).

Stanley Wolpert, a senior American India-specialist of the University of California in Los Angeles, takes the matter somewhat further:

> This was the most important invasion in all of India's history since the Aryans brought with their Caucasian genes a new language – Sanskrit and a new pantheon of gods (Wolpert 1997: 27).

Genes, language and culture (here described as 'a new pantheon of gods'), have been nicely combined here in one sentence. The term 'Aryan' has by no means lost its shades of ugliness even in the modern context. As Bruce Lincoln puts it,

> Since the atrocities of the Nazis in the Second World War, the term 'Aryan' has virtually disappeared from polite conversation. Scholars who wish to pursue the old discourse while marking their distance from its less savoury aspects now use the term "(Proto-)Indo-European," also a coinage of the nineteenth century. In doing so, many sincerely believe that they have thereby sanitized the discourse and solved the problems, but things are not so simple. Often such euphemizing attempts are incomplete, superficial, evasive, and disingenuously amnesiac (Lincoln 1999: 94-95; I owe the reference to A. Ananth Kumar's article in http://www.India-forum.com, "The AIT: more than meets the eye").

That the premises related to the Proto-Indo-European language, its homeland, etc. are not objective 'science' has been illustrated well by E.F.K. Koerner (www.tulane-edu/howard/langldeo/koerner/koerner.html) with reference to linguistic historiography in general and by C.M. Hutton with reference to his study of *Linguistics and the Third Reich: Mother-tongue Fascism, Race and the Science of Language* (Hutton 1999; I owe the references to Koerner and Hutton to A. Ananth Kumar's article). In Koerner's analysis,

> ... the field must learn to accept that linguistics, past and present, has never been 'value free', but has often been subject to a variety of external influences and opinions, not all of them beneficial to either the discipline itself or the society that sustains it.

Koerner argues that implicit ideological underpinning was embedded even in the first nineteenth century proposals of linguistic typology. It is also useful to remember here what Bruce Lincoln writes about the reconstruction of a 'protolanguage':

> In specific, reconstructing a "protolanguage" is an exercise that invites one to imagine speakers of that protolanguage, a community of such people, then a place for that community, a time in history, distinguishing characteristics, and a set of contrastive relations with other protocommunities where other protolanguages were spoken. For all this, need it be said, there is no sound evidentiary warrant (Lincoln 1999: 95).

The history of the last two hundred years of Indo-European scholarship has been analysed recently by Stefan Arvidsson who has shown how the idea has been intimately linked with the various social and political processes and ideologies and how unsafe it would be to construct historical images on that basis (Arvidsson 2006).

The Indo-European premise exposed itself fairly clearly when some mummies of the second and first millennia BC were found in the Tarim basin of the Taklamakan desert of Chinese central Asia. The Wikepedia article on the Tarim mummies categorises them clearly as "Caucasoid mummies", apparently Europeans or Indo-Europeans, if one prefers, on their way to China. In an essay titled "Hidden discourses of race: imagining Europeans in China" (homepages.utoledo.edu/nlight.uyghhst.htm), Nathan Light points out the eagerness and delight with which these mummies have been seized upon as 'proof' of Indo-European migration to China.

The Sarasvati project issue also seems to have got completely out of hand. The Parliamentary Committee's view notwithstanding, it is not a mythological river, and a close study of the entire drainage system related to it is in fact vital to understand the transition from the Indus to the early historic traditions of the upper Ganga plain and the Indo-Gangetic divide. For reasons not clear to the present author, its course was traced in some recent literature up to Kutch and Kathiawad. I am not sure how the Sarasvati course could have gone into the peninsular Gujarat, although I admit that this region could have been affected by the declining fortunes of the Sarasvati flow as the combined flow of the Indus and the Sarasvati joined the sea in the present day area of the Rann of Kutch. The geological data were no doubt assessed for this project, but it appears that the project did not get sharp enough archaeological focus. One does not know why the sites of Bhirrana, Adi Badri, Baror, Juni Kurn, etc. were selected for excavations and what these excavations would have told about the ancient flow of the Sarasvati. However, the attempt of its critics to relate the project itself to the RSS version of ancient India or to dub it "anti-Dravidian" in intentions is logically worse than some of the exaggerations of its champions. It is indeed unfortunate that a government-sponsored research programme on the river which is traditionally considered to include in its valley some of the holiest areas of Hinduism should be subject to what has to be considered a purely political dispute – a dispute in which one has to take a stand in the name of 'progress' versus 'reaction'.

If one has to comment on the research aims of such organizations as "World Association for Vedic Studies", one has to say straightaway that our knowledge of ancient India is unlikely to be augmented by putting emphasis only on Vedic studies.

Alternative pathways to the study of ancient India must be consciously sought and pursued. By making the Vedas the prime focus of our study we are unlikely to get anywhere, although the enumeration of various technical concepts immanent in this body of text is a valid exercise. But as far as historical reconstruction is concerned, the Vedas are unlikely to open any new door. The historical value of a corpus of traditions which have accumulated over possibly many centuries and carry terms which are open to a wide range of interpretations is unlikely to be great. The scientists, technologists and other professionals who are motivated enough to set up an organization for a better study of ancient India should try to move away from the image of an India where the key principles are generally related to spiritualism. There is a vast field of material India which needs close regional and local level studies, and it is here that the professional expertise of the expatriate Veda enthusiasts may be of considerable use. Regarding the Vedas, whatever we may say about them cannot be brought down to a rigorous chronological frame, and without a suitable chronological frame it is hardly of great use historically. The so-called 'Vedic Age' is a chimera, nothing more than the summation of what can be gleaned from the amorphous and possibly very incomplete mass of texts known as the Vedas.

In our second chapter we began by pointing out certain aberrations in Indian Stone Age research – strongly marked group loyalties, lack of an all-India perspective, etc. They may be partly due to the fact that this research, with some exceptions, has not, by and large, matured in India, and remains unrelated, except in a vague way, to the history of India. Organizing a multi-disciplinary geoarchaeological group comprising geology, sedimentology, pedology, lithic artefact technology, landscape archaeology and spatial analysis for Stone Age research is not an easy job in an Indian university or other institutional set-ups, and archaeologists are very often reduced to doing what they can do themselves, i.e., the discovery of sites and observations on stratigraphy and typology. Even where some geological support is available, the support in most cases is very basic. For instance, the fact that a particular industry can be related to a particular geological 'formation' is unlikely to tell us anything about the conditions in which this 'formation' was formed and the specific environmental and other contextual data in which the relevant 'industry' emerged and functioned. Considering the fact that the archaeologist concerned is usually from the Humanities stream, eventually what one gets is a kind of geological 'leavening' to spruce up an otherwise monotonous succession and spread of lithics. This is in no way intended to pull down Stone Age research in India, but merely a cautionary note to have a proper sense of perspective in this field.

In this chapter we have also pointed out that Indian archaeologists, historians and those who are concerned with the way in which the subcontinent has got populated show a marked reluctance to accept the notion of India being the centre of any major cultural or technological development and innovation. From this point of view, the study of Indian archaeology may be considered somewhat unique, because it cannot be easy to find parallels of this attitude among the historians and archaeologists anywhere. We have cited three main Indian authors – H.D. Sankalia, V.N. Misra and M. Gadgil (and his associates), and one foreign scholar, Elizabeth Rosen Stone, in this connection. Are they isolated examples of scholarship or do they reflect a general trend? These opinions were picked up at random, but if further examples are necessary, one may cite from a publication dated 2006.

In a survey of the changes which took place in ancient India between the Mauryas and the Guptas, Harry Falk of Free University, Berlin, divides its history into four phases. The Mauryas (320 BC-c. 185 BC) dominated the first phase when Hellenistic culture was spreading widely and its most important king Asoka was "eager to introduce elements of western culture, be it script or well-maintained road systems". The phase which followed has been called "indigenous" and includes the rule of the Sungas, Kanvas, Mitras, Dattas and others. They were "children of the soil" and had little contact with the western cultures in their time-bracket of c. 185-c. 50 BC. The third phase is initiated by intruding westerners, be they of Iranian, Scythian, or Kushana stock". They spread themselves over most of north India. The fourth phase began with their dispersal and culminated in the rule of the Guptas. According to Falk, this is a phase marked by "a dispersal of foreign rule and the return to traditional values". Falk's summing up of these 600 or 700 years of India's ancient history is the following:

> Roughly speaking, the Mauryas made use of the Hellenistic brain drain; the succeeding Sunga dynasty and its successors shunned intense foreign contacts; instead, traditional grammar and ritual were revived.
>
> The succeeding foreign rulers of Saka, Pahlava, and Kushana stock neglected the indigenous way of life and built centres of learning, e.g. at Ujjain, and made a living through intensive trade relations with East and West. The succeeding Gupta Dynasty reverted to indigenous values, to sciences of the word; inspiration from foreign sources began to come to a close. The oscillating pattern could be described as an alternation between an interest in the exact sciences and the science of letters; it could be described as a recurring shift between religious plurality and conservative henotheism and monotheism. At least to us, today, the recognition of new foreign elements seems to be an indicator of a positive attitude toward innovation (Falk 2006: 146).

Falk's attitude is clear enough: only those phases which had foreign domination and contacts are considered 'innovative' phases by him. For instance, he thinks that the Mauryan art started with "stonework inherited from Achaemenid Iran". Soon his tone turns political and reveals his attitude to modern India (or India of April 2004 when the conference where this paper was read took place):

> Presently, since partition, India seems to be gradually moving back to another phase of introspection. Despite the thriving IT business in Bangalore, the main change observable to an outsider concerns the Hinduttva ideology. Traditional values like the caste system are again being cherished as fundamental, foreign religions and attitudes are under attack. On the other side, the Vedic sacrifice in all grades of debasement is spreading rapidly, even into corners which would have been regarded as impure in earlier times. When will the BJP or some other traditional force perform the first national Asvamedha? (Falk 2006 146-147).

The relationship between the author's attitude to ancient India and his perception of modern India is clear in this passage. This article is interesting in the sense that this relationship is usually kept covert and not made as explicit as this.

In the same conference where Falk read his paper, F. Asher read his paper on early Indian art (Asher 2006). His attitude to those who maintain that the Asokan pillars are "purely Indian" in spirit is plainly sneering. He calls it "a refrain maintained in much writing on Indian art, even to the present, for those who continue to wage a nationalist campaign" (Asher 2006: 54). To scholars like Falk and Asher, nationalism in the context of the study of ancient India is only something to be sneered at.

Among the Indian scholars N.R. Ray in his book *Maurya and Sunga Art* was unequivocal about his opinion that the Mauryan art was inspired by the Achaemenid art. He also accepted the idea that the style of Asokan inscriptions was modelled on the corresponding Achaemenid style. This Achaemenid inspiration was in fact central to his argument that the Mauryan court art was a glass-house creation which fell apart immediately after the disintegration of the Mauryan empire.

It is thus apparent that the attitude we have read in Sankalia, Misra and Gadgil (and his associates) is not an isolated attitude limited to only a handful of scholars. It is much more widespread than that, and cuts across a vast cross-section of scholars, both Indian and foreign. Again, we have to revert to the theme of colonial Indology as the prime frame of this attitude.

In our third essay we have tried to identify the focal points of the sociopolitics of the study of the Indus civilization. The main battle these days seems to be between those who believe that the Indus or Harappan people – whoever they were – spoke a language (or languages) of the Indo-Aryan family and those who believe that this language belonged to the Dravidian family in general and was Tamil in particular. As we have seen, the debate goes back to 1924, the year when the discovery of the civilization was announced.

The question whether the people of this civilization spoke an Indo-Aryan language or not involves in turn the question of its relationship with the Vedic literature. Here also the scholarship is sharply divided. To John Marshall, it was pre- and non-Vedic, but he did not specifically invoke the Dravidians either. R.P. Chanda before him tried to account for the Indus phenomenon within the frame of the Vedic literature, arguing initially a phase, however brief, of interaction between the two. In this phase of his thought Chanda squarely held that the Indus cities with their fortifications were destroyed by Indra of the Rigveda. In the second phase of his research Chanda was more keen to find interrelationships, postulating that the Indus kings were influenced by the Rigvedic priests and eventually found place in the Rigvedic society and later as the *Kshatriyas* or warrior caste. He also found echoes of Indus people in some Rigvedic groups of people like the Panis. More significantly, Chanda traced the roots of the later *Dhyana-Yoga* in the *Sramana* figure from Mohenjodaro and thought that the civilization antedated some forms of Hinduism, Buddhism and Jainism. In this sense Chanda was the first scholar to relate the Indus civilization to the High Tradition of the Vedic and later India.

That the Indus civilization was within the fold of the Vedic literature, both early and late, was argued by two great scholars of their time – Bhupendra Nath Datta in 1936-37 and Pandurang Vaman Kane in 1953. Datta's approach was mainly anthropological and directed mainly at the refutal of the notion that there had to be long-headed fine-nosed skeletons in the Indus skeletal assemblage to denote the Aryan presence in that civilization. Citing some of the foremost anthropologists of that period and before, Datta ridiculed the prevailing Indian scholarly opinion that only the 'Nordic skulls' would indicate the presence of the Aryans and opined that the Alpinoid brachycephalic element, which in any case was present among the Mohenjodaro skeletons, would do nicely as well. Another major part of Datta's argument rested on the Vedic parallels of the Indus burial methods – complete inhumation, fractional and post-cremation burials. For this he depended mostly on the evidence of the disposal of the dead at Harappa which had undergone by this time fairly extensive excavations under M.S. Vats who himself later on cited Vedic analogies for some of the paintings that he reported on the Cemetery H pottery of the site. Datta was not happy with Max Muller's dating of the Rigveda; he appreciatingly cited M. Winternitz's opinion that the Rigveda's date was uncertain and could well date from c. 3000 BC. Neither was he happy with the suggestion that the Rigvedic terms *Dasas* and *Dasyus* denoted non-Aryans.

P.V. Kane as a Sanskritist did not find anything commendable in Max Muller's dating of the Rigveda. The supposed philological similarities with the equally supposed late date of the Avesta did not cut any ice with him. Basing himself mainly on the astronomical references in the Vedic literature, which would suggest for it a long time-span from c. 6000 BC onward, he argues the chronological situation of both the Indus civilization and the Vedic literature being fluid, there could not be any decision regarding the interrelationship between the two on the basis of chronological considerations. Further, he argues that there were inter-group rivalries between the different groups of Aryans and that the occupants of the Indus fortified cities could represent one or more of these groups. He also points out the importance of bull and *Pipal* in the Rigveda and draws attention to their significance in the Indus civilization. It appears that Kane prefers to leave the issue open, because he comments on the inadvisability of dogmatising on this problem. At the same time, he finds nothing objectionable about the idea that the Rigveda could be earlier than the Indus civilization.

As we have pointed out, the modern concern with the so-called Vedic affiliation of the Indus civilization got heightened only after a limited area in the dried-up Sarasvati valley came to be recognized as the epicentre of this civilization. Considering the pre-eminence of this valley in the Indian sacred tradition, it is but natural that this concern will now be more widespread than it was before. B.B. Lal's monograph *And the Sarasvati Flows On* or S.P. Gupta's *Indus-Saraswati Civilization* should be viewed in this context. Equally importantly, the image of the Rigveda as depicting a non-urban agricultural and pastoral society began to undergo a distinct change, first in Bhagawan Singh's *Vedic Harappans* and then in R.S. Bisht's citation of the Vedic sources to highlight the three-fold division of Dholavira town-planning. If the Rigveda and the later Vedic literature cover a very long tradition, it is not surprising that this should contain references to various stages of society from the simple to the complex. Perhaps the issue is not entirely settled, but there does not seem to be any point in such opinion as R.S. Sharma's that the Bactro-Margiana Archaeological Complex entered India and created the Rigveda. Nor is there any weighty consideration in D.N. Jha's statement that the Rigvedic Aryans were fair-skinned and conscious of it. The advantage of having an extensive and highly polemical debate on the internet over this issue is that it is a wide open field now where everybody can say his or her own piece. That a fairly innocuous controversy like this should generate so much heat was possibly unimaginable before the internet moved in. There are exaggerations on both sides, but behind all this turbulence lies a world of long-standing scholarship, and it would be invidious to dub it purely as a battle between ' reaction and progress' or between 'communalism and secularism'. One does hope that scholars of the stature of R.P. Chanda, B.N. Datta, P.V. Kane and others who do not find any essential dichotomy between what has been portrayed in the Vedic literature and the Indus civilization would not invite the epithet 'Hindu fundamentalist' from any quarter. All of them are no more guilty than having challenged the received wisdom; one very often forgets that challenging the received wisdom is one of our academic tasks.

In comparison, the Tamilian point of view has been rather poorly served. S.K. Chatterji could hardly go beyond the orthodox language classification and language history of India where the speakers of the Dravidian languages moved to their present distribution zone from elsewhere, having come to India in the first place from an indeterminate area stretching as far west as the Mediterranean. His reference to the cultural traits of modern Hindu worship or *Puja* being Dravidian in origin is not particularly edifying, especially because he offers no argument whatsoever in this case. What is somewhat distressing is that this point of view became a kind of emotional issue among a certain section of Tamilian population, Sumathi Ramaswamy's analysis being a sharp pointer in this direction. Gurumurty's attempt to bring archaeology to the dispute, which we have quoted, cannot be called a success. However, this is in no way meant to rubbish the Tamilian theory. For all one knows, the Harappan language may turn out to be Tamil, although for this, as for claiming that the Harappans spoke and wrote an earlier form of Sanskrit, the Harappan script has to be deciphered first to everybody's satisfaction.

What is more important is that there is evidence that south India was within the orbit of the Harappan tradition. Even if one ignores the issue of Karnataka and Tamil Nadu raw materials such as Kolar gold or Nilgiri amazonite being drawn into the Harappan commercial network, one cannot ignore the evidence of the Neolithic celt inscribed with Harappan signs or the more solid evidence of upper Ganga plain copper hoard implement of antennae-hilted sword which is now found to belong to an indisputable Harappan tradition, late or otherwise, being found as far south as southern Tamil Nadu and Kerala. Moreover, there is the still unclear question of a burial at Dholavira where the pit was found lined with stone slabs, a typical south Indian megalithic trait. Indications of stones being arranged in circles on the top of burials have also been reported from elsewhere in the Harappan context of Gujarat. The point is that the Aryan/Dravidian controversy should not be seen as an emotive issue in the Indus context but as a fair academic debate where the opinion of the other side has to be appreciated without converting it into a battle between reaction and progress.

It is quite natural that something as vast and complex as the Indus civilization should be studied from a whole range of perspectives. The famous *Siva-Pasupati* seal from Mohenjodaro, despite its apparent male form including ithyphallic state, has been identified by a scholar as a female deity (Atre 1987), but disputes of this kind are not something which should distort our total perspective.

There is absolutely no justification to refer to this civilization by a geographically inaccurate term such as the Indus valley civilization. The civilization did not originate in the Indus valley but in a limited segment of Cholistan. Both Indus valley and Cholistan are in Pakistan; so there is no special point to call it the Indus valley civilization to give it a special Pakistan angle. There is also no justification at all in claiming that this development lies at the end of an arrowline beginning with the development of wheat-barley-cattle-sheep-goat domestication at Mehrgarh in Baluchistan. The difference in time between the two relevant points is enormous, and meanwhile the Aravallis (and possibly Gujarat) have emerged as one of the focal points of early agricultural and metallurgical development, setting the ground, so to speak, of the development of 'Early Harappan' over a vast zone to the east. Further, at some point, rice and millets got added to the Early Harappan crop-list and gave it an agricultural complexity which could not be discerned before. The unlineal emphasis on wheat-barley cultivation as forming the base of the Indus civilization is only a device to link it to the so-called Middle Asia sphere. The way in which the evidence of rice and millets in the Early Harappan is ignored in a certain type of archaeobotanical literature is amazing, to say the least, and underlines once again that there is a steady refusal to consider this civilization as a purely subcontinental phenomenon in certain quarters.

The main battle of the sociopolitics of the study of the Indus civilization lies in fact in this direction: whether the Indus civilization forms the base of the Indian High Tradition, as earlier scholars like Marshall, Chanda and Kane never tired of emphasizing. To many of us, the distribution of the Indus sites is best understood with reference to the historical roles of these areas in later Indian history. For instance, I have emphasized (Chakrabarti 2004) that in the ancient context Mohenjodaro possibly fulfilled the same function which the trading emporium of Shikarpur fulfilled in the nineteenth century. Both were located in the area where the trade across the Bolan pass debouched into the Indus plain. The question is what we look for. Do we try to understand the nature and mechanism of Indus external trade in the frame of the network of trade that linked more or less the same areas till recently and was something in which the mercantile communities of Sind and elsewhere in the northwest played a leading role, or do we visualise it only with reference to a few bits of evidence in the Mesopotamian textual sources and highlight the whole thing as exerting a determinative influence on the transition from the Early Harappan to the Mature Harappan? Opinions will differ, and Indian scholars have been as enthusiastic as some non-Indian ones to discover the key to the Harappan universe in its external trade. Shireen Ratnagar's famous conclusion that the Indus civilization came about and flourished mainly to supply raw materials to Mesopotamia (Ratnagar 1981) finds a good echo in what M.K. Dhavalikar wrote about the reason of Harappan presence in Gujarat:

> The locational analysis of Early Mature Phase settlements in Gujarat leads one to conclude that initially the Harappans were not interested in colonising Gujarat, their sole objective being the exploitation of resources which were not available in Sindh and Punjab. This would explain why they located their settlements mostly in the coastal areas, and even those which were in the interior were established for the same purpose. The Harappans do not seem to have made any conscious effort in the acculturation of the autochthones. The latter seem to have been living in shanties outside the fortified settlements as at Kuntasi.

> It is indeed surprising that in all the two or three centuries of the Early Mature Harappan phase the number of their settlements did not grow beyond twenty-five even in such a vast area. They can therefore be compared with the European imperialists in Africa, particularly the Portuguese and the Belgians, who exploited the colonies to the maximum without making any attempt to ameliorate the lot of their subjects. *They would have continued to do so but for the tremendous spurt in the demand for Indian goods in Mesopotamia* (italics added). This attracted people from Sindh and hence new areas in Saurashtra were occupied. The degeneration set in from ca. 1900 BC because of decline in trade and in consequence people had to resort to pastoral nomadism and seasonally settled life. Later still in some places they resorted to hunting-gathering (Dhavalikar 1995: 100).

How does Dhavalikar know that there was suddenly a 'tremendous spurt in the demand for Indian goods in Mesopotamia'?

Elsewhere he writes that in the beginning the Harappans only made forays in Gujarat, settled at places like Kuntasi and acquired raw materials, passing them on to Sindh and Punjab to be processed into finished goods.

> But with increase in demand for some oriental luxuries such as ivory and semi-precious stones like carnelian, it was thought more profitable to manufacture the articles in Gujarat itself and export them to West Asia. This was the stage when the fortified settlements such as those of Surkotada, Pabumath, Desalpur, Kuntasi, etc. were built for affording protection to itinerant merchants-traders (Dhavalikar 1995: 181).

Apparently, Dhavalikar holds the fate of the Gujarat Harappans hostage to west Asian trade. He even refuses to consider that the vast Harappan region covering about the western one-third of the subcontinent could generate its own demand for raw materials on a vast scale.

It is time we accepted the idea that the Harappan civilization does not represent a vast monolithic growth but suggests the background presence of multiple, possibly regional, traditions which eventually coalesced into the form that we know as the Early and Mature Harappan, and shared with this complex, in varying proportions, some of its dominant (or at least visible) traits. Instead of a monolithic political entity, we should see it as a cluster of different polities of different sizes in various parts of its distribution zone. Meanwhile, we should not be ashamed to claim that its religion, art, crafts, economy, agriculture and possibly even ideology still continue to influence the subcontinent's life in various ways. We must not also try to denigrate it by putting forward only those slices of data which suit our individual theories and ignoring those which do not. In recent years, a good example of this has been provided by Shireen Ratnagar in her book *The End of The Great Harappan Tradition* (Ratnagar 2000) where she argues that the Harappan decline might be linked to its "dependence on imports of metals". On the other hand, the first thing that one realizes while studying Harappan metallurgy is that the Harappan distribution area is particularly rich in metals including copper and tin. It did not have to depend on the import of metals from outside its own area.

The very fact that the Harappan chronology has been found to be more wide than was previously thought has made it easier to appreciate it as a long cycle of purely Indian development, albeit with close contacts with the contemporary world. One remembers that as late as 1982, the emphasis was on a short chronology for this civilization – 600-odd years for both the nuclear and peripheral areas, and for the nuclear area only a spread of about 200 years (Agrawal 1982: 188). Such a short chronology has the sub-text of portraying it an ephemeral phenomenon in Indian history, something which can be considered a mere flicker. Today the Early to Late Harappan time-span is roughly from 3500 BC to 1300/1400 BC, and beyond this on the early side streches the long phase of the Hakra ware which, going by the recent Bhirrana dates, falls in the 5th millennium (if not the 6th millennium) BC. With such a spread of its history, only the most biased would try to relate its inspiration to Middle Asia.

The issues of our fourth essay deal primarily with the confusions and uncertainties regarding the chronology of the beginning of the early historic period in the subcontinent. A historiographical background may be necessary to understand the case. In terms of the political history of ancient India, it was the *Mahajanapada* period, the period when the subcontinent was divided into a number of major principalities, sixteen of which have been mentioned in the Buddhist literature, with a number of others occurring in the Jaina literature and other sources. Basically, it was considered the period of the Buddha, for whom the general chronology was c. 543-c. 463 BC, with variations of some years. The major city – sites which were excavated in the first-half of the twentieth century were mostly the capital cities of these principalities, which were also associated in some cases, as in the cases of Rajgir, Vaisali, Sravasti and Kausambi, with prolonged phases of the life of the Buddha. These were also places which were mentioned in the Buddhist *Jatakas* and other literature. On the whole, there was a rounded image of the beginning of early historic India tied to the life of the Buddha in the sixth century BC and the Buddhist literature which was taken to reflect the condition of that period. This was the picture which Mrs. C. Rhys Davids portrayed in *Buddhist India*. The specific dates of the beginning of writing and coins were not investigated in detail, but it was taken for granted that there must lie some centuries of development behind the third century BC marker of Asokan inscriptions, and as far as the coins are concerned, the Buddhist literature extensively mentions them as well as the wide prevalence of writing.

The problem began when the NBP came to be considered the diagnostic ceramic marker of the beginning of the early historical phase in the Ganga plain and put between the fifth and second centuries BC, completely ignoring Marshall's early dating of it in the eighth century BC. In fact, one is not sure if there was even an awareness of this dating by Marshall before 1988 when the present author pointed this out. The problem became more muddled when it was assumed that the find of the NBP outside its core area could only mean its expansion with the expansion of the Mauryan empire and thus dated it considerably later than its original date in the Ganga valley. Along with this lowering of the date of the NBP, there was also a re-questioning of the date of the Buddha and putting it down 100-odd years later. As far as the beginning of writing is concerned, scholars went to the extent of claiming that it was Asoka who deliberately introduced writing in the subcontinent and thus dating this development not earlier than the third century BC. The same thing happened more or less with the coins, although in this case it got tagged with the date of the NBP, in which level the coins occurred first. The net result of all this was that the beginning of the early historic period in India lost its earlier sharp picture, and occasionally one comes across opinions which put primary focus on the Maurya period (cf. Monica Smith 2006, defining the chronological span of early historic cities from c. third century BC to fourth century AD) in this connection. From our point of view it is a sacrilege to ignore the urban history of India before the third century BC.

A number of things have clearly emerged in recent years. The NBP can now be placed in the eighth century BC in the central Ganga plain, which also should be the date of the first coins. Secondly, it is understood that the date of the NBP outside its core area need not coincide with the spread of the Mauryan rule; it could be much earlier and move along the trade routes soon after it came into existence in the Ganga plain. Thirdly, the attempts to lower the date of the Buddha have fizzled out, because such claims were also made before. The basis of the sixth century BC date for the Buddha may not be cast iron but it fits the available evidence on the whole. Fourthly, it has been realized that attacking the generally accepted early dates of the Buddhist tradition incorporated in the early Buddhist literature such as the *Jatakas* may be off the mark. A sixth-fifth century BC date may safely be assumed for the historical tradition contained in them. Finally, there is no serious academic reason to deny that the use of script on perishable material in India began as early as the eighth century BC. On the whole, we seem to have gone back to our earlier image of the beginning of the early historic period in the subcontinent. I, for one, find no reason to feel apologetic about it.

I have clearly put forward the case for early dating of Tamil-Brahmi inscriptions in Tamil Nadu. As far as I can judge, the scholars who refuse to put them before the third century BC have not been able to put forward their chain of argument clearly, and until that view-point can be examined in detail, the beginning of writing at Kodumanal and elsewhere should be given the date of at least c. 500 BC.

Another debate that I have outlined here relates to the supposed significance of the beginning of iron in ushering in the phase of second urbanisation in the subcontinent. The debate has been definitive in the sense that there is now not a shadow of evidence to argue that the history of iron technology in India can be divided into a number of 'modes'. For instance, ploughshare occurs in the very first phase of the beginning of iron at Malhar around 1800 BC. Malhar is in the eastern fringe of the Kaimurs near Banaras, and soon afterward iron occurs extensively at Dadupur near Lucknow and other sites in the central Ganga plain. Considering that the early historic cities did not emerge till about 800 BC, there is a history of about a thousand years of iron-use behind it. Only a very dogmatic person would now insist that the use of iron was the most important causative factor behind the growth of these cities.

Having gone through the material that I have cited and discussed in this volume, I am forced to wonder why some of India's most eminent scholars of ancient India should display in print such a low opinion of their subcontinent's ancient past. That it is not an isolated opinion is shown by the range of scholars that we have picked up quite arbitrarily and who cover a large spectrum of scholarly attitudes and beliefs – H.D. Sankalia who laid the foundations of archaeological research in the Deccan College, Pune; V.N. Misra, a noted prehistorian and a former Director of the same institute; Irfan Habib, a noted scholar of Mughal India, a former chairman of that regulatory body of historical studies in India, Indian Council of Historical Research, and a leading public spokesman of the Indian Left's point of view in historical issues; and finally, M. Gadgil and his associates with interest in the population history of India. These scholars, all reputed and secure in their own domains in the country, are unanimous in denying any technological or innovative originality to the ancient past of the land which has sustained them. Further, in any explanatory scheme, they simply jump at any opportunity to link the problem under enquiry with something external. M.K. Dhavalikar as the excavator of Inamgaon will always have an important place in the history of Indian archaeology, but there is no point to ignore his explanation of why the Harappan settlements expanded in Gujarat. According to him, the Harappan settlements increased in number in Gujarat because the Harappans decided to process Gujarat's raw materials into processed goods in Gujarat itself and export these goods to Mesopotamia in response to a spurt in the quantum of trade between the two regions. That there is no conceivable evidence to suggest such a 'spurt' in the concerned trade at this point could not deter him from linking Harappan expansion in Gujarat with a causative mechanism rooted elsewhere. That Dhavalikar ascribes to the Harappans in Gujarat the role of the early European colonists in India is interesting too in its own right. Gujarat and Sindh are two neighbouring regions, with traditional links throughout history. Dhavalikar's hypothesis implies that Gujarat herself played no role in the formation of the character of the Indus civilization there. Should the seeds of regionalism be carried as far back as protohistory? Of course, Dhavalikar's is not an isolated opinion. One has only to think of the way in which Indo-Roman trade has been found to lie at the base of all prosperity in India of the early centuries AD.

I certainly consider it tragic that so much of our public concern should be focussed on the Aryan issue in various forms – the Sarasvati river, the Aryan invasion/migration theory, the Vedas and so on. Even while welcoming the intense debates on them, I would say that such issues do not add by themselves anything new or significant to our understanding of ancient India. History, as we all know, has been enacted on land, and how much of our ancient land and its interaction with History that we know? While gazing outside a moving train's window, we may occasionally think of the passing landscape and ask ourselves how much do we know of the location and character of the past human settlements and life in that landscape. Very often I realized that I either knew very little or nothing at all This simple fact may tell us that a very vast amount of what can be known about ancient India remains unknown, and there is absolutely no way we can touch the past shadows unless we go out to that land and investigate. That we are not very historically minded is also clear from the fact that only a small percentage of the total collections of our museums is put on display. According to Nayanjot Lahiri (2006) only 8 to 10% of the total collection of the National Museum in Delhi is on display, and even that too in an uncatalogued state. The Indian Museum in Calcutta has only 1165 archaeological collections on display whereas more than 25000 objects lie locked in storage there.

One does not have to be a trained archaeologist to investigate the past human traces in the land; in many countries ordinary men and women have played a leading role in investigating their land's past. Even in the subcontinent one can think of dedicated people in various professions quietly pursuing their historical investigations at the ground level. In Britain, for instance, such investigations have always been a passion with people, and the literature which has been built on the basis such investigations is a pillar of academic support for the professional community of historians and archaeologists. From this point of view, it is indeed unfortunate that the only historical issues which excite us Indians as a body – expatriate or otherwise – is such issues as the coming of the Aryans or Dravidians. We do not even realize that such issues – the issues which have to infer about the existence or non-existence of a particular language or language-family in a non-literate context – are virtually unknowable by any standard of logic. This lack of realization on our part is to a great extent due to the textual image that we have built of our ancient past – a land of wise sages who were far more advanced in their thoughts than their contemporaries elsewhere in the world. This is why highly educated Indian professionals set up societies to promote the study of the Vedas and the Vedic thoughts. This is why we fight to the ground over whether the people behind these Vedas were indigenous or came from outside, and to people to whom the Vedas are only reminiscent of Hindu ideology or political Hindutva, the people who set them down or memorized could only be invaders, having as much right in the Indian soil as any other group of invader. Why should the authorship of the Indus civilization be something very important for the Tamil identity or their pride in being speakers of the Tamil language? After all, the speakers of this language had many other things to be proud of in their history. Many of such issues are inexplicable and got mixed up in a curious way with the brand of "progress versus reaction" politics, but what this development clearly suggests is that the historical thought-process of the Indians got inexorably skewed in a wrong direction – the direction of linguistic and ethnic/racial affinities, or, if one prefers, the direction of colonial Indology. This attitude has permeated various levels of our historical consciousness and even in the colonial period it was not limited only to the representatives and allies of the colonial power. The Indian historians of the day tried to combat this only in individual cases; the basic structure was not generally challenged. This basic structure is still there. We have cited Falk's notion that innovative phases of early Indian history are only those with foreign contacts and influences. More or less the same attitude has been displayed by the Indian scholars we have cited at various points. Archaeology is as much affected by it as ancient history. The time it has taken for the significance of the Aravallis as an early centre of agriculture and metallurgy with implications in the Harappan studies to sink in the Indian archaeological literature is a convenient example. For many years a somewhat blind support for the late date of the NBP gave a somewhat distorted chronological perspective to everything related to the beginning of early history in the Ganga plain. The reluctance to see the obvious, i.e., an earlier date, in the case of Tamil-Brahmi inscriptions in Tamil Nadu is another case in point. It is apparent that the need to wage nationalist battles is not yet over in ancient Indian studies.

One of the reasons of the still prevailing importance of the colonial Indological attitudes is that ancient Indian studies including archaeology are marginalised in Indian education and society. As is well-known, the Indian society does not actually encourage the study of those subjects which are not 'modern', i.e., do not command a good value in the job market. What one has eventually got is somewhat somnolent university and college departments in such subjects – departments which actually do not much encourage students to think independently. Rajiv Malhotra has emphasized that, whereas the study of Greek and Roman Classics is acknowledgedly an important part of the curriculum of many Western higher centres of learning, the study of Indian classics is neglected even in India. It is not neglected in the sense that Sanskrit is not widely taught in Indian schools, colleges and universities. In fact, it is taught quite widely. However. The Sanskrit teaching set-ups in India invariably suffer from the general stigma of being backward-looking, and the fact that Sanskrit is not compulsorily taught at the school level in many places has meant that the modern Indian students' ability to appreciate the roots of their mother-tongue has remarkably declined.

Another likely reason is the persistence of the old colonial frame of thought in relation to India in the field of humanities and social sciences in many Western universities and academic bodies. Rajiv Malhotra has critically examined the issue and described it as "the axis of neo-colonialism". One of his comments in this connection throws socio-political light on the scholarly opinions we have discussed in this volume.

> While each rich and powerful civilization emphasizes its indigenous cohesiveness and continuity, and with scholarship under control of those loyal to it, the reverse is the trend among the economically weak civilizations such as India. In the case of

> the Indian civilization, the scholar's emphasis has been on how there might not even be such a historical entity as India or Hinduism, and how its civilization was entirely brought by foreigners into India. This intellectual break-up of the Indic Traditions into historical layers of cultural imports, each with a nexus in some other part of the world, is the intellectual equivalent of the political breakup of India. That so many Indians have sold out to this project is certainly noteworthy and is a major untold story of our times (Malhotra, 'the axis of neocolonialism' in Sulekha.com Blogs, 2002).

In another article in Sulekha.com Blogs ('RISA Lila – 1. Wendy's child syndrome' 2002) Rajiv Malhotra discusses the scholarly attitudes to the majority religion of India, Hinduism, in the portals of the American scholarly association, Religions in South Asia. This is mostly an internal analysis, beginning with an examination of an American scholar's premise that Sri Ramakrishna Deva (1836-1886), the famous Kali-worshipping mystic of nineteenth century Calcutta, whom many Indians consider as an incarnation of God, and his famous disciple Swami Vivekananda (1863-1902) had an unnatural relationship. The point to remember about this type of scholarship is that much of it is usually based on active research cooperation of Indians and that except in such extreme examples, the so-called scholarly theories in question are not even critically examined by Indians in most cases. The Western scholarship in Indian Studies of various kinds has got used to getting away by writing almost anything on India, and unless Indian scholars acquire some self-respect, which is not an easy thing to do, considering the ramifications of 'fellowship network', this is unlikely to change. Many of these 'fellowships', more or less earmarked for Third World scholars in Western universities, are usually controlled by the subject experts of those universities, who look around and select only those who possess, according to them, potential and promise of various kinds. The Western 'India experts' with powers to pull strings in fellowship selections are generally considered demi-gods in the Indian academic context, with the young (and old) hopefuls milling around them in every lecture and conference. Mr. Malhotra need not worry about the way the majority Indian religion is viewed in the Western academia; it is a well-known thing.

In 2001, while trying to understand the archaeology of Hinduism, I pointed out a comment by H. Von Stietencron, an

Indological scholar from Tubingen (Chakrabarti 2001). According to him there was no Hindu religious unity before the nineteenth century, and this concept of Hindu religious unity was mistakenly built up by the British by lumping the Vishnu and Siva worshippers together. Later on, this concept was necessary to build up an Indian national identity.

> This, indeed, is a case where nationalist politics in a democratic setting succeeded in propagating Hindu religious unity in order to obtain an impressive statistical majority when compared with other religious communities. *It is a manipulated majority which would certainly appear much less dominating, if the two largest communities in present-day India, the Vaishnavas and the Saivas, would be recognized as having distinctly separate, though culturally cognate, religious origins* (italics added, Stietencron 1995: 52).

The scholar's attitude is quite clear; he thinks that the fact that Hinduism is the majority religion of India has been due only to a quirk of the British rulers who lumped worshippers of Siva and Vishnu together. Interestingly, this attitude was in no way a hindrance to his being honoured with a *Padmasri* by the Government of India on the Republic Day of 2004. The government in Delhi on that day was NDA government with BJP as the dominant partner.

In the context of Rajiv Malhotra's analysis, a few elementary points deserve consideration from the Indian point of view. First, the western scholars will research their subject in the light of the prevailing western academic perspective regarding India. They have no reason to consider the Indian perspective in their field. Secondly, this research is pursued, not specially because the scholar concerned likes India or her people but because to him/her this is a career choice. If there is a tradition of contempt for Indian perspective or scholarship in Indian studies in the academic context he/she comes from, there is no reason why the scholar concerned should try to go beyond it. Thirdly, why should Indians expect that the person in question will not write something which is offensive to Indians? In an article entitled "academic researchers versus Hindu civilization" (Sulekha.com Blogs, December 9, 2004) Gautam Sen had as its objective "to understand why Indian studies in the West ... are overwhelmingly hostile to their object of study". One of the reasons which he does not discuss is a large scale compliance of the Indian professionals in this matter.

In the field of archaeology some Western scholarly opinions have been considered in this volume, and such opinions do not emanate only from the Western archaeological community but from some Indians as well. Unfortunately, the division between the Western scholars doing Indian archaeology and their Indian cohorts, and the general Indian archaeological community is getting sharper. The following opinion of mine may reflect the current situation:

> If this reviewer's Indian experience is anything to go by, the current crop of Euro-American archaeologists working in India is far more contemptuous of the native archaeological scholarship, arrogant, and dependent on the hand-wringing of local lackeys than the full-blooded colonial archaeologists ever were at any point in India's colonial history (Chakrabarti 2006a).

Our neighbouring country Pakistan has had a better luck in this regard. I can think of at least two groups, one British and the other French, which built up over the years an excellent research tradition in Bannu and Baluchistan, without telling in print all and sundry what wonderful research they were doing and how bad was the Pakistani archaeological scene till they appeared with their superior intellect there. It would be difficult to think of any such decent foreign archaeological group in modern India.

The contempt for the native scholarship is clearly conveyed by the fact that in any discussion on an Indian archaeological issue in the western archaeological literature, the Indian opinion seldom figures in the general theoretical discussion on the problem. The element of arrogance is personal and comes through in general interaction. The 'local lackeys', who must remain nameless in the present context, can be easily identified in the Indian archaeology departments by the people familiar with the subject and its literature including websites.

This unfortunate situation, which should not be tolerated by the sensible scholars on both sides, has come about mainly because of two developments in international archaeology. First, instead of the Western archaeologists who used to spend a lifetime by studying the archaeology, history and culture of a geographical region and were familiar with the different nuances of life there, we have increasingly people who are not interested in an area *per se* but are committed to test their theories about various things in a wide global context. To them, the locals are just necessary evils – minor irritants – in their quest for grand theories. Secondly, modern archaeological research is widely science-based, something that most of us Indian archaeologists cannot cope with. The foreign teams in Indian archaeology invariably depend on multidisciplinary inputs, and that is a contrast with most of the Indian groups which depend on excavations, their knowledge of the land and whatever limited scientific analytical facilities they have access to. There is an in-built element of tension always between the two groups. Thirdly, a great part of the Western archaeology that gets to work in India is 'anthropological archaeology', and its protagonists, both Indians and Westerns, never tire of lecturing others that this is the best way to approach the study of the past. The reason why this approach has failed to make any serious impact on the Indian scene is that the 'anthropological archaeologists' have not been able to come up with explanations or perspectives which were beyond the intellectual range of ordinary history-trained archaeologists like us. What is increasingly noticeable these days is that a theoretically oriented publication will begin with a template which will say how wonderful a particular theory is to explain the archaeological problem in hand. No case-study will be necessary to drive the point of its importance home. The next section will deal with the archaeological data very much on their own, and in the final section, it will be re-emphasized how helpful has the induction of the theory which is mentioned in the opening section been to understand the archaeological scenario. Scholars who still set some store by empirical research, which many of us Indians do, can only feel amused, if not irritated. For instance, there is nothing of 'anthropological archaeology', different protestations notwithstanding, in invoking Bactrian parallels for the so-called seals of Gilund. It is exactly this kind of comparison which Sankalia invoked for the designs on Ahar beads many years before. Or, I might draw attention to what J.G. Shaffer has postulated on Hakra ware, the archaeological tradition of the Ganga plain and the Tibetan plateau. He has derived the entire subcontinental complex under consideration from the direction of Tibetan plateau (Shaffer 1992: 437-438). The point is that the anthropological archaeologists have generally been unable to contribute anything significant to the study of ancient India, despite their liberal use of anthropological jargons in this field. If one is expected to cite some modern examples, I would cite two articles in the 'South Asia' issue of *Asian Perspectives* (42.2, 2003), one on the identification of the Chera, Chola and Pandya kingdoms in south India by Shinu A. Abraham (2003) and the other on the Asokan inscriptions in south Deccan by N. Sugandhi (2003). Not a single interesting point about ancient Indian history can be said to have emerged out of these writings, despite their long anthropological protestations. Fourthly, the Western archaeologists, even when writing on areas outside their own lands, write in the context of the academic tradition which has been built up for that area in the Western academia. They are not concerned with what the academic tradition of the area concerned will think of it, nor are they particularly concerned with the literature which has emanated from that quarter on this theme. Below the veneer of polite academic facade, there is always a sneering attitude to the native scholars, which is best seen in 'confidential' manuscript and grant proposal evaluations.

In an article entitled "repositioning India's brand" (rediff.com, December 9, 2003) Rajiv Malhotra comments that the US academia related to India abounds in 'negative stereotypes':

> Anti-progress:
> Indian culture is depicted as primitive, obsolete, and frozen until outsiders come and push it forward. Hence, the implication seems to suggest, we must invite outsiders to come and fix problems for us.
>
> Unethical:
> Indian culture is essentialized by images of abusive caste, sati, dowry deaths, and other human rights atrocities, including aggressive charges of fascism, violation of minority rights and violence. Indian scholars often lead these parades that overemphasize public tirades against India in the West, while failing to understand the implications of brand damage in a global capitalist system.
>
> Unscientific:
> Indians are shown as mystical people lacking Western style rationality.

> Everything good about India is assumed to have been imported: The British gave us a sense of nation. There was no worthy Indian culture prior to the Mughals. The Greek brought philosophy and mathematics to India. The "Aryans" brought Sanskrit. By implication, Indians are doomed to dependency, which contradicts the vision of India's future trajectory being based on knowledge-based industries.
>
> Many Indian scholars in the humanities, journalists, and "intellectuals" in Non-Government Organizations depend on Western funding, Western sponsored foreign travel, acquiring legitimacy in the eyes of Western institutions, the ability to parrot canned Western 'theories', and even identifying as a member of the Western Grand Narrative (not as options but as necessary conditions for success). Clearly such loyalties, identities and ideologies must resonate with their sponsors.

In another of his articles Rajiv Malhotra poses the question "does South Asian Studies undermine India" (rediff.com, December 4, 2003) and states (in the context of the United States) that "serious academic scholarship about India is rarely in the hands of scholars with loyalty to India". No loyalty is necessary or called for, but what is needed is an open mind and some willingness to look at the Indian point of view without sneer – unfortunately features which are conspicuously lacking in the Western academia related to India. There are certainly honourable and distinguished exceptions, but their presence only highlights the situation we have discussed.

In this context it may be useful to remember what P.V. Kane wrote more than 50 years ago:

> European historians writing about matters Indian were obsessed by several considerations such as race prejudice, ideas of the 'white man's burden', scorn for Indians who were frequently invaded and conquered and who were deemed not to have ever possessed high intellectual attainments or originality in anything. To such feelings we must attribute the various theories trotted out by western historians from time to time; for example, one may refer to Dugald Stewart's outburst that the whole Sanskrit literature was a fabrication of the wily brahmanas from Greek sources made centuries after Alexander (vide Vol. III of his works, edited by Sir William Hamilton, pp. 78-115); that the Ramayana was inspired by Homer's Iliad, that the Gita was based on the Bible, that writing was unknown to Panini, that the

> Brahmi script was borrowed from the Phoenicians, that the ancient Indian system of *nakshatras* was borrowed from the Chinese or the Arabs or some people in Western Asia, particularly the Babylonians (Kane 1953: 4).

Elsewhere in the same publication he comments:

> Speaking with the greatest respect for the industrious and learned scholars of the West I cannot help observing that their conclusions are extremely one-sided and that they have often built huge structures on very meagre foundations and made too much of a very disputable evidence and it is to be regretted that many western writers and Indian scholars also have blindly followed in the wake of the pioneers and added their own imaginary conclusions without carefully and cautiously weighing the evidence offered and the probabilities (Kane 1953: 9).

Some Indian ancient historians may not even be ready to consider any other alternative of looking at ancient Indian history. In *Colonial Indology: Sociopolitics of the Ancient Indian Past* I tried to offer one such alternative in which "all Indians, irrespective of their individual affiliations can feel having a share": "... it is time we focussed on the story of the land itself, the story of how human groups, irrespective of their biological, linguistic, cultural and religious affiliations, have eked out a livelihood out of this land" (Chakrabarti 1997: 239). This point of view has been criticized by B.D. Chattopadhyay, a leading ancient historian of India "as the desire for a dangerous, single-dimensional nationalist agenda of writing about the past; it does not seem to admit that all Indians may not find it possible to subscribe to one 'alternative sense' of the past. Secondly, as I argue in the text, Indian past, or any other segment of human history for that matter, cannot be the exclusive preserve of a single 'indigenous' perspective for the simple reason that no such perspective has ever existed" (Chattopadhyay 2001: 15).

If Chattopadhyay had bothered to find out about the various archaeological and natural-scientific techniques of working out the history of land, he would certainly have realized that the end-result does not advocate a 'single-dimensional' perspective, nationalist or otherwise. The issue here is not to offer a single-dimensional hegemonic view of the past but to offer a perspective based on the human interaction with the land, which does not have any place for the tenets of colonial Indology and their modern continuation. Further, as Chattopadhyay must be aware, the history of nationalism and archaeology in various parts of the world demonstrates that a nationalist or 'indigenous' perspective of approaching archaeology is not an 'unheard of' phenomenon.

The concept of 'national archaeology' is not unknown either. Beatrice Fleury-Ilett (1993) points out that the idea of 'Archaeologie nationale' in France has three characteristics: (1) it builds on the existence of separate archaeologies, such as Palaeolithic archaeology, classical archaeology and mediaeval archaeology, in the French soil, by giving equal weight to the intervening periods as well and by attempting to address the total as a coherent whole; (2) it is not synonymous with French archaeology because that includes French archaeologists involved in other parts of the world; (3) it is distinct from any area outside France, although the area may be archaeologically related to France. It is said that 'archaeologie nationale' and the centrally run organization of archaeology in France make it 'particularly susceptible to political and ideological trends'. It is also worth quoting the following comment by the Danish archaeologist Kristian Kristiansen:

> In Europe we tend to moralise over the Third World's neo-nationalism, but we entirely forget our own, which came about in exactly the same way, and still thrives for better or worse. The problems seem in fact to be growing at the present time, especially in countries with several ethnic or national groups which do not wish to be integrated (Kristiansen 1992: 18).

Archaeology in India, if it has to carve out a wide intellectual base for itself in the country, has to be concerned primarily with national history. We have not focussed on our 'national archaeology' yet, but it is high time we did so.

Like its predecessor *Colonial Indology, Sociopolitics of the Ancient Indian Past*, this volume also has ended up by being a polemical work, something which points out the sub-texts of the different strands of the sociopolitics of Indian archaeology. I believe that polemics of this kind is something very necessary if the archaeological study of the ancient Indian past has to understand itself and realize its true potential. In a different context, I deeply appreciate what a Chicago professor of English wrote in 1993:

> Not that Western knowledge can simply be replaced by existing non-western forms, but that one can look for new structures

that combine and transcend what already exists. In that case the task of the writer, critic, or journalist would be one of continued questioning, not only of the Western tradition but also, in the manner of one disposed to learning, of non-western traditions and their transformations in a post-colonial world. To avoid intellectual quietism, this writing would have to run the risk of epistemic violence encountered in all striving toward new knowledge ... The Moroccan writer Abdelkabir Khatibi observes that the decolonization of the Third World has not brought about a corresponding decolonization of thought which would be, apart from a simple reversal of colonial power, the "affirmation of difference", an openness to plurality and a free subversion of the powers that inhere in discourse. The work of deconstructing colonial discourse is even greater than that of dismantling the massive systems of colonial administration; it is a work that has only just begun, to say nothing of the creation of entirely new discourse (Spurr 1993: 200).

Appendix

DANCING TO WHOSE TUNE ?

Among the manifold achievements of the Archaeological Survey of India (ASI), the discovery of the Indus civilization is justifiably the crowning glory. It could declare in 1924 that like Egypt and Mesopotamia, India, too, had one of the earliest civilizations of the world. Moreover, unlike Egypt and Mesopotamia, where the credit of discovery goes entirely to foreign expeditions and where the responsibility of interpreting it rested wholly with foreign scholars, the Indian story is essentially Indian. This was presided over by John Marshall, the Director General of the ASI between 1902-31, whose *Mohenjodaro and the Indus Civilization* (1931) still remains the most authoritative exposition of the framework of this civilization.

The fact that its roots lay deep in the subcontinental soil or that it foreshadowed many later elements of the Indian civilization, including its art, religion and many material forms, was very clearly emphasised in this volume. What emerges strongly in Nayanjot Lahiri's recent archivally researched *Finding Forgotten Cities*, on the discovery of the Indus civilization, is the element of strong teamwork of the archaeologists of the ASI behind this momentous discovery and their intellect and professional commitment that put them on par with the more well known names in the global history of archaeological discoveries.

The ASI carried the story forward with equal degree of professional commitment after Independence. With Mohenjodaro and Harappa both going to Pakistan, it was imperative that the evidence of the fountainhead of Indian civilization should be found within the confines of modern India. The officers of the ASI rose equal to the task, swiftly mapping out not merely the extensive distribution of this civilization in Gujarat, Rajasthan, Punjab, Haryana and western UP but also throwing important light on the history of its development in these areas.

On the whole, two facts stand out. First, there is not a shadow of doubt that the Indus civilization is as pristine and autochthonous as any other civilization of the Old World. And second, it is by no means synonymous with the Indus valley and thus cannot be called the 'Indus Valley Civilization'. In retrospect, it is educative that Marshall called it the 'Indus civilization' without relating it exclusively to the Indus valley.

It is important at this point to draw attention to a well-researched theme of modern archaeology, i.e., the issue of the 'socio-politics' of the past. The basic point is that our approach to the past is controlled by various characteristics of the society to which we ourselves belong. The Ayodhya and Bamiyan incidents in the recent past are clear enough proofs of this point.

In the socio-politics of the Indus studies, the current international scholarship has a sub-text that is academically unacceptable to Indian archaeologists. The sub-text is that the Indus civilization is related essentially to 'Middle Asia' in inspiration and not to South Asia as such. The archaeological evidence is overwhelmingly to the contrary but that has not deterred Euro-American archaeologists from pressing this point in various forms and guises.

This does not really affect Pakistan because the area from the Oxus valley to the Indus valley is one interaction zone, and to this extent Pakistan may be visualised as a part of 'Middle Asia'. The term 'Indus Valley Civilization' puts the civilization firmly in the context of Pakistan alone. However attractive the term is to our Pakistani colleagues, we Indians cannot accept it, first because the civilization extends far beyond the Indus valley, and second because there is as yet no acceptable evidence that the civilization belongs in any sense to the middle or central Asian orbit.

It is also important that we refer to an unpleasant but inescapable phenomenon of global archaeological research, i.e., the element of tension between First World and Third World archaeologies. With some honourable but regrettably rare exceptions, the archaeological research by First World archaeologists in the Third World is currently characterised by plain insolence – a complete contempt for whatever has been done in the field of archaeology in that part of the world by indigenous archaeologists. The fact that a number of indigenous archaeologists are invariably manipulated by such First World archaeologists by throwing different types of 'carrots' to them makes the situation rather sordid from the Third World point of view.

As far as India is concerned, the post-Independence archaeological leadership of the country was astute enough to understand these implications of allowing unrestricted access to international archaeologists to Indian sites. It is because of this that the opinion of Indian scholars still matters in the domain of Indian archaeology. However amazing it may sound, this simply is not true of an overwhelmingly large part of the Third World, where First World archaeologists call the shots.

What is worrying is that the country's archaeological leadership is now in doldrums. The ASI has been without a professional leadership for more than a decade, and the less we look at the details of its current working the better. However, it is precisely in such moments that long-term national interests in the field get forgotten and things are made easy for the unscrupulous.

The recent announcement of the establishment of an 'Indus Centre' in Gujarat under the auspices of the M.S. University, Baroda, and Global Heritage Fund, a California-based funding organisation, seems to be a textbook illustration of such scenarios. The detailed analysis of the backgrounds of the archaeologists (both Indian and American) concerned is not hope-inspiring, but more specifically, I am alarmed by the implicit arrogance of their letter of announcement of the Centre.

First, it declares that this 'Centre' aims to conserve "Indus valley's most important archaeological sites", all of which are incidentally in Pakistan, because that is where, with the exception of the Ladakh part of the valley, the Indus valley lies. It is most unlikely that the Pakistan government will hand over the responsibility of conserving "Indus valley's most important archaeological sites" to this Centre in Gujarat! Apparently, this 'aim' is nothing but a ruse to impress the gullible.

Second, the arrogance behind the announcement that the 'Centre' intends to set up "India's first world-class museum and research institute for education, tourism and scholarship on the Indus valley civilization" is amazing. It clearly implies that whatever has been done in the field of Indus civilization, studies in India so far are below the level which the organisers of this 'Centre' consider to be world-class.

Third, the letter consistently uses the term 'Indus Valley Civilization', a term which, as we have earlier pointed out, is both academically incorrect and politically unacceptable.

Fourth, this 'Centre' is the first foreign-funded archaeological institute in India, ostensibly to take care of one of the most crucial dimensions of our heritage. It has serious long-term implications, and before the authorities gave it the green signal, the matter ought to have been openly discussed in the country's professional bodies of archaeology. As things stand, we do not even know who took the decision and under whose pressure.

India's Indus heritage has a long and assured history of research and work. Why is it that we are today turning a Nelson's eye to this and behaving as if we can't survive without foreign saviours? Why are we so demoralised that we must outsource a crucial part of our heritage in this way?

Note: the foregoing article was published in *The Hindustan Times* of Delhi on January 2, 2006. That my concern in this matter is not irrelevant is shown once again by the circular issued by another Global Heritage Fund expert, Professor Michael Tomlan of Cornell who introduces himself as the Director of Hampi Foundation. The tone of the circular , which announces a conference and workshop entitled "Taking Vijayanagara's Past into the Future" at Hampi on January 19-20, 2008, clearly implies that the initiative of whatever research has so far been done on the Vijayanagara capital has a strong 'American' angle, and the purpose of the conference now is to make the locals realise the significance of this site and the American or America-sponsored research on it.

> As you know, a number of academic conferences and discussions have taken place in the last few years regarding the history and the future of Hampi World Heritage site. Museums and academic institutions in Los Angeles, Houston and Mumbai have served as admirable hosts. Meanwhile, some of the regional administrators, archaeologists, architects, contractors, craftsmen, and people in Karnataka are just now beginning to learn the remarkable amount of information that has been assembled. Meetings with local residents and stakeholders have begun regarding the changes that will take place.

As far as ordinary Indian archaeologists are concerned, the lead role in the excavations of Hampi has always been taken by the Archaeological Survey of India which is also responsible for the upkeep and protection of this monument. Its status as a World Heritage Site does not take away the role of the Survey in this matter. We are aware that the 'Vijayanagara Past' has long been nurtured as a kind of separate enclave by some of our foreign and Indian colleagues without trying to relate it to the contemporary forces and features of Indian history. What is somewhat alarming that now there is a concerted attempt to turn the issue of its conservation also into another detached enclave blessed apparently by such organisations as Global Heritage Fund. One wonders how many enclaves of this type that one will soon find in Indian archaeology and how many 'circulars' of this kind that one has to put up with in future.

Bibliography

Abraham, Shinu A. 2003. 'Chera, Chola, Pandya: Using Archaeological Evidence to Identify the Tamil Kingdoms of Early Historic South India', *Asian Perspectives* 42: 207-223.

Agrawal, D.P. 1982. *The Archaeology of India*, London: Curzon Press.

——. 1992. *Man and Environment in India through Ages*, Delhi: Books and Books.

Agrawal, D.P. *et al*. 1995. 'Cist-burial of the Kumaun Himalayas', *Antiquity* 69: 550-554.

Arvidsson, S. 2006. *Aryan Idols: Indo-European Mythology as Ideology and Science*, Chicago: University of Chicago Press.

Asher, F.M. 2006. 'Early Indian Art Reconsidered', in P. Olivelle (ed.), *Between the Empires, Society in India 300 BCE to 400 CE*, New York: Oxford University Press, pp. 51-66.

Atre, S. 1987. *The Archetypal Mother – A Systematic Approach to Harappan Religion*, Pune: Ravish.

Banerji, R.D. 1922-23. 'Western Circle, Sind, Mohenjodaro', *Annual Report of the Archaeological Survey of India* 1922-1923, pp. 102-104.

Bergunder, M. 2004. 'Contested Past, Anti-Brahmanical and Hindu Nationalist Reconstructions of Indian Prehistory', *Historiographia Linguistica* 31: 59-104.

Bisht, R.S. 1988. 'Some Glimpses of Mercantile and Maritime Activities of the Rigvedic Aryans', in S.R. Rao (ed.), *Marine Archaeology of Indian Ocean Countries*, Dona Paula (Goa): National Institute of Oceanography, pp. 12-13.

——. 1989-90. 'Dholavira: New Horizons of the Indus Civilization', *Puratattva* 20: 71-82.

Braidwood, R.J. and Wiley, G.R. (eds.). 1962. *Courses toward Urban Life*, Chicago: Aldine.

Bryant, E. 2001. *In Quest of the Origins of Vedic Culture: The Indo-Aryan Migration Debate*, New York: Oxford University Press.

Bryant, E. and Patton, L. (eds.). *The Indo-Aryan Controversy: Evidence and Inference in Indian History*, London: Routledge.

Childe, V.G. 1944. 'Archaeological Ages as Technological Stages', *The Journal of the Royal Anthropological Institute of Great Britain and Ireland*, pp. 7-24.

Chakladar, H.C. 1936. 'Problems of the Racial Composition of the Indian People', *Man in India* 16: 99-134.

Chakrabarti, Dilip K. 1972-73. 'Concept of Urban Revolution and the Indian Context', *Puratattva* 6: 27-32.

——. 1977. 'India and West Asia: An Alternative Approach', *Man and Environment* 1: 25-38.

——. 1968. 'The Aryan Hypothesis in Indian Archaeology', *Indian Studies: Past and Present* 9: 343-358.

——. 1973. 'Beginning of Iron and Social Change in India', *Indian Studies: Past and Present* 14: 329-338.

——. 1976. 'The beginning of iron in India', *Antiquity* 50

——. 1986. 'Further Notes on the Aryan Hypothesis in Indian Archaeology', in K.C. Varma *et al.* (eds.), *Ritambhara, Studies in Indology*, Ghaziabad (Kavinagar), pp. 74-75.

——. 1988. *Theoretical Issues in Indian Archaeology*, Delhi: Munshiram Manoharlal.

——. 1988. *A History of Indian Archaeology from the Beginning to 1947*, Delhi: Munshiram Manoharlal.

——. 1990. *The External Trade of the Indus Civilization*, Delhi: Munshiram Manoharlal.

——. 1997. *Colonial Indology: Sociopolitics of the Ancient Indian Past*, Delhi: Munshiram Manoharlal.

——. 2000. 'Colonial Indology and Identity', *Antiquity* 74: 667-671.

——. 2001. 'The Archaeology of Hinduism', in T. Insoll (ed.), *Archaeology and World Religion*, London: Routledge, pp. 33-60.

——. 2003. *Archaeology in the Third World: A History of Indian Archaeology since 1947*, Delhi: DK Printworld.

—— (ed.). 2004. *Indus Civilization Sites in India – New Discoveries*, Mumbai: Marg Publications.

——. 2006. *The Oxford Companion to Indian Archaeology. The Archaeological Foundations of Ancient India. Stone Age to AD 13th Century*, Delhi: Oxford University Press.

——. 2006a. 'Review', *Journal of the Royal Anthropological Instutute* NS 12: 963.

Chakrabarti, Dilip K. and Lahiri, Nayanjot. 1994. 'The Iron Age in India: the beginning and consequences', *Puratattva* 24: 12-32.

——. 1996. *Copper and Its Alloys in Ancient India*, Delhi: Munshiram Manoharlal.

Chanda, Ramaprasad. 1929. *Survival of the Prehistoric Civilization of the Indus Valley*, Calcutta: Memoir of the Archaeological Survey of India, No. 41.

——. 1926. *The Indus Valley in the Vedic Period*, Calcutta: Memoir of the Archaeological Survey of India, No. 31.

Chatterji, S.K. 1924. 'Dravidian Origins and the Beginnings of Indian Civilization', *The Modern Review* (December issue): 665-679.

Chattopadhyay, B.D. 2001. *Historical Perspective and Its Distortion*, Jaipur: Institute of Rajasthan Studies.

Dales, G.F. 1964. 'The Mythical Massacre at Mohenjodaro', *Expedition* 6: 36-43.

Danino, M. 2004-2005. 'Dholavira's Geometry: A Preliminary Study', *Puratattva* 35: 76-84.

Das, A.C. 1925. 'Dravidian Origins and the Beginnings of Indian Civilization, *Modern Review*, March issue, pp. 355-357.

Datta, B.N. 1936-37. 'Vedic Funeral Customs and the Indus Valley', *Man in India* 16:223-307, 17: 1-68.

Dever, W.G. 1998. 'Archaeology, Ideology, and the Quest for an "Ancient" or "Biblical" Israel', *Near Eastern Archaeology* 61: 39-51.

Dhavalikar, M.K. 1997. *Indian Protohistory*, Delhi: Books and Books.

——. 1995. *Cultural Imperialism. Indus Civilization Sites in Western India*, Delhi: Books and Books.

Diamond, J. and Bellwood, P. 2003. 'Farmers and their Languages: The First Expansions', *Science* 300 (5619): 597-603.

Diaz-Andreu, M. 2004. 'Britain and the Other: The Archaeology of Imperialism', in R. Phillips and H. Brocklehurst (eds.), *History, Identity and the Question of Britain*, New York: Palgrave, pp. 227-241.

Diaz-Andreu, M. and Champion, T. (eds.). 1996. *Nationalism and Archaeology in Europe*, London: University College London Press.

Dikshitar, V.R. Ramachandra. 1947. *Origin and Spread of the Tamils: A Course of Two Lectures Delivered under the Sankara-Parvati Endowment, University of Madras*, Adyar: Adyar Library.

Elst, K. 1999. *Update on the Aryan Invasion*, Delhi: Aditya Prakashan.

Falk, Harry. 2006. 'The Tidal Waves of Indian History: Between the Empires and Beyond', in P. Olivelle (ed.), *Between the Empires, Society in India, 300 BCE to 400 CE*, New York: Oxford University Press, pp. 145-166.

Fleury-Ilett, Beatrice. 1993. 'The Identity of France: The Archaeological Interaction', *Journal of European Archaeology* 1.2: 169-180.

Fowler, D.D. 1987. 'Uses of the Past: Archaeology in the Service of the State', *American Antiquity* 52: 229-248.

Ghosh, A. (ed.). 1989. *Encyclopaedia of Indian Archaeology*, Delhi: Munshiram Manoharlal.

Golla, V. *et al.* 2003. 'Response', *Science*, 28 May, 2003.

Guha-Thakurta, Tapati. 2002. 'For the Greater Glory of Indian Art: The Life of an Endangered Art Treasure in Modern India', *International Journal of Cultural Property* 11: 1-27.

Gupta, S.P. 2000-2001. 'River Saraswati in History, Archaeology and Geology', *Puratattva* 31: 30-38.

Habib, I. 2001. *People's History of India 1, Prehistory*, Delhi: Tulika.

Harke, H. 1998. 'Archaeologists and Migrations, A Problem of Attitude', *Current Anthropology* 39 (1): 19-45.

Hutton, C. 1999. *Linguistics and the Third Reich: Mother-tongue Fascism, Race and the Science of Language*, Chicago: Chicago University Press.

Jayaswal, V. 1982. *Chopper-Chopping Components of Palaeolithic in India*, Delhi: Agam Kala Prakashan.

Jha, D.N. 1998. *Ancient India in Historical Outline*, Delhi: Manohar.

Jha, S.K. 1998. *Beginnings of Urbanization in Early Historic India, a Study of the Gangetic Plains*, Patna: Novelty and Co.

Kak, S.C. 2006. 'Vedic Astronomy and Early Indian Chronology', in E.F. Bryant and L. Patton (eds.), *The Indo-Aryan Controversy, Evidence and Inference in Indian History*, London: Routledge, pp. 309-331.

Kane, P.V. 1953. 'Presidential Address', *Indian History Congress, Proceedings of the Sixteenth Session: Waltair*, pp. 1-18, Calcutta: Indian History Congress Association.

Kennedy, K.A.R. 2003 (reprint). *God-Apes and Fossil Men: Palaeoanthropology in South Asia*, Ann Arbor: University of Michigan Press.

Kenoyer, J.M. 2002. 'Challenges in Pakistan, Efforts to Combat a Taliban Mentality: An Interview with J. Mark Kenoyer', *Archaeology* (March-June issue), pp. 19-21.

——. 2006. 'New Perspectives on the Mauryan and Kushana Periods', in P. Olivelle (ed.), *Between the Empires, Society in India, 300* BCE *to 400* CE, New York: Oxford University Press, pp. 33-49.

——. 2006a. 'Culture Change During the Late Harappan Period at Harappa, New Insights on Vedic Aryan Issues', in E.F. Bryant and L. Patton (eds.), *The Indo-Aryan Controversy, Evidence and Inference in Indian History*, London: Routledge, pp. 21-49.

Khandalavala, K. 1988. 'The Didarganj *Chauri*-bearer: Another View-point', *Lalitkala* 23: 12-13.

Kochhar, R. 2000. *The Vedic People: Their History and Geography*, Hyderabad: Orient Longman.

Kohl, P. 1998. 'Nationalism and Archaeology: On the Constructions of Nations and the Reconstructions of the Remote Past', *Annual Review of Anthropology* 27: 223-246.

Kohl, P. and Fawcett, C. (eds.). 1995. *Nationalism, Politics and the Practice of Archaeology*, Cambridge: Cambridge University Press.

Kosambi, D.D. 1956. *An Introduction to the Study of Ancient India*, Bombay: Popular Prakashan.

——. 1965. *The Culture and Civilization of Ancient India in Historical Outline*, London: Routledge and Kegan Paul.

Kristiansen, Kristian. 1992. 'The Strength of the Past and its Great Might: An Essay on the Use of the Past, *Journal of European Archaeology* 1: 3-32.

Lahiri, Nayanjot. 2005. *Finding Forgotten Cities. How the Indus Civilization was Discovered*, Delhi: Permanent Black.

——. 2006. 'Beyond the Brussels Blitz, Ringside View', *The Hindustan Times*, 18 November.

Lal, B.B. 1953. 'Protohistoric investigations', *Ancient India* 9: 80-102.

——. 2005. *In Search of the Aryan Homeland – The Continuation of a Debate*, Delhi: Aryan Books International.

Lal, M. 1986. 'Iron Tools, Forest Clearance and Urbanisation in the Gangetic Plains', *Man and Environment* 10: 83-90.

Lincoln, B. 1999. *Theorizing Myth: Narrative, Ideology and Scholarship*, Chicago: Chicago University Press.

Londo, J.P. *et al.* 2006. 'Phylogeography of Asian Wild Rice', *Oryza rufipogon* Reveals Multiple Independent Domestications of Cultivated Rice', *Proceeedings of the National Academy of Sciences*, USA 103(25): 9578-9583.

Mahadevan, I. 1984. 'The Cult on Unicorn Seals: A Sacred Filter?', *Puratattva* 13-14: 165-186.

——. 2003. *Early Tamil Epigraphy. From the Earliest Times to the Sixth Century* AD, Chennai: Cre-A.

Marshall, J. 1923-24. 'Exploration and Research, Harappa and Mohenjodaro', *Annual Report of the Archaeological Survey of India*, 1923-24, pp. 47-56.

—— (ed.). 1931. *Mohenjodaro and the Indus Civilization*, London: Arthur Probsthain.

Meskell, L. 2002. 'The Intersections of Identity and Politics', *Annual Review of Anthropology* 31: 279-301.

—— (ed.). 1998. *Archaeology under Fire, Nationalism, Politics and Heritage in the Eastern Mediterranean and Middle East*, London: Routledge.

Misra, V.N. 1970. 'Cultural Significance of three Copper Arrow-heads from Rajasthan, India', *Journal of Near Eastern Studies* 29: 221-231.

——. 1989. 'Stone Age India: An Ecological Perspective', *Man and Environment* 14(1): 17-64.

——. 2001. 'Prehistoric Human Colonization of India', *Journal of Bioscience* 26: 491-531.

Misra, S.S. 2006. 'The Date of the Rigveda and the Aryan Migration, Fresh Linguistic Evidence', in E.F. Bryant and L. Patton (eds.), *The Indo-Aryan Controversy, Evidence and Inference in Indian History*, London: Routledge, pp. 181-233.

Mohapatra, G.C. 1985. 'Cultural Ecology of Early Man in India', in S.B. Deo and K. Paddayya (eds.), *Recent Advances in Indian Archaeology*, Pune: Deccan College, pp. 23-38.

Nagaswamy, R. 1993. 'The Dravidian Problem – Epigraphic Sources', in S.B. Deo and Suryanath Kamath (eds.), *The Aryan Problem*, Pune: Bharatiya Itihasa Sankalana Samiti, Maharashtra, pp. 84-85.

Oppenheimer, S. 2004. 'The Express Train from Taiwan to Polynesia: On the Congruence of Proxy Lines of Evidence', *World Archaeology* 36(4): 591-600.

——. 2006. 'Response to Peter Bellwood and Jared Diamond (2005): On Explicit "Replacement" Models in Island Southeast Asia: A Reply to Stephen Oppenheimer', *World Archaeology* 38(4): 715-717.

Poliakov, L. 1974. *The Aryan Myth, a History of Racist and Nationalist Ideas in Europe*, London: Chatto, Windus Heinemann.

Possehl, G.L. 1990. 'Revolution in the Urban Revolution: The Emergence of Indus Urbanization', *Annual Review of Anthropology* 19: 262-282.

——. 1996. *Indus Age, the Writing System*, Delhi: Oxford Book Store and IBH.

Possehl, G.L., Shinde, V. and Ameri, M. 2004. 'The Ahar-Banas Complex and the BMAC', *Man and Environment* 29 (2): 18-29.

Potts, D. 2005. 'A Note on Post-Harappan Seals and Sealings from the Persian Gulf', *Man and Environment* 30(2): 108-111.

Radhakrishna, B.P. and Merh, S.S. (eds.). 1999. *Vedic Sarasvati: Evolutionary History of a Lost River of Northwestern India*, Bangalore: Geological Society of India.

Radhakrishnarao, K.V. 1993. '"Ariyar" in Ancient Tamil Literature', in S.B. Deo and Suryanath Kamath (eds.), *The Aryan Problem*, Pune: Bharatiya Itihasa Sankalana Samiti, Maharashtra, pp. 75-80.

Ramachandran, K.S. 1980. *Archaeology of South India; Tamil Nadu*, Delhi: BR Publishing Corporation.

Ramaswamy, Sumathi. 2001. 'Remains of the Race: Archaeology, Nationalism, and the Yearning for Civilization in the Indus Valley', *The Indian Economic and Social History Review* 38: 105-145.

Rangarajan. 1993. 'Aryan Dravidian Racial Dispute from the Point of View of Sangam Literature', in S.B. Deo and Suryanath Kamath (eds.), *The Aryan Problem*, Pune: Bharatiya Itihasa Sankalana Samiti, Maharashtra, pp. 81-83.

Rao, S.R. 1993. 'The Aryans in Indus Civilization', in S.B. Deo and Suryanath Kamath (eds.), *The Aryan Problem*, Pune: Bharatiya Itihasa Sankalana Samiti, Maharashtra, pp. 173-180.

Rapson, E.J. 1914. *Ancient India*, Cambridge: Cambridge University Press.

Ratnagar, S. 1981. *Encounters*, Delhi: Oxford University Press.

——. 2000. *The Great Harappan Tradition*, Delhi: Manohar.

Ravi Prasad, G.V. *et al.* 2006. 'AMS Facility at Institute of Physics, Bhuvaneswar: Inter-laboratory Comparison of Results', *Current Science* 90(4): 488-490.

Rosser, Yvette. 1983. *Curriculum as Destiny: Forging National Identity in India, Pakistan and Bangladesh*, Ph.D thesis, University of Texas at Austin.

Sahoo, S. *et al.* 2006. 'A Prehistory of Indian Y Chromosomes: Evaluating Demic Diffusion Scenarios', *Proceedings of the National Academy of Sciences*, USA 104(4): 843-848.

Sahu, Bhairavi Prasad (ed.). 2004. *Iron and Social Change in Early India*, Delhi: Oxford University Press.

Sankalia, H.D. 1973. 'Prehistoric Colonization of India', *World Archaeology*: 86-91.

——. 1977. *Prehistory of India*, Delhi: Munshiram Manoharlal.

——. 1978. *Born for Archaeology: An Autobiography*, Delhi: BR Publishing Corporation.

Sarma, I.K. 1972. 'South-east Asia, India and West Asia', in S.B. Deo (ed.), *Archaeological Congress and Seminar Papers*, Nagpur: Nagpur University, pp. 95-112.

Schlumberger, D. 1988. 'The Didarganj *Chauri*-bearer: A View-point', *Lalitkala* 23: 9-11.

Shaffer, J.G. 1992. 'Chapter 26', in R. Ehrich (ed.), *Chronologies in Old World Archaeology*, Chicago: University of Chicago Press.

Sharma, R.S. 1983. (2001 reprint). *Material Culture and Social Formation in Ancient India*, Delhi: Macmillan.

——. 1999. *Advent of the Aryans in India*, Delhi: Manohar.

Silberman, N.A. 1998. 'Whose Game is it Anyway? The Political and Social Transformations of American Biblical Archaeology', in L. Meskell (ed.), *Archaeology under Fire. Nationalism, Politics and Heritage in the Eastern Mediterranean and Middle East*, London: Routledge.

Singh, B. 1995. *The Vedic Harappans*, Delhi: Aditya Prakashan.

Smith, Monica L. 2006. 'The Archaeology of South Asian Cities', *Journal of Archaeological Research* 14: 97-142.

Smith, V. 1889. 'Graeco-Roman Influence on the Civilization of India', *Journal of the Asiatic Society of Bengal* 58: 107-198.

——. 1924. *Early History of India*, Oxford: Oxford University Press.

Spence, Kate. 2000. 'Ancient Egyptian Chronology and the Astronomical Orientation of Pyramids, *Nature* 408: 320-324.

Spurr, David. 1993. *'The Rhetoric of Empire, Colonial Discourse in Journalism, Travel Writing, and Imperial Administration*, Durham: Duke University Press.

Sridhar, T.S. (ed.). 2005. *Alagankulam, an Ancient Roman Port City of Tamil Nadu*, Chennai: Department of Archaeology, Government of Tamil Nadu.

Steitencron, H. von. 1995. 'Religious Configurations in pre-Muslim India and the Modern Concept of Hinduism', in V. Dalmia and H. Steitencron (eds.), *Representing Hinduism*, Delhi: Sage Publications, pp. 51-81.

Sugandhi, N. 2003. 'Context, Content, and Composition: Questions of Intended Meaning and the Asokan Edicts', *Asian Perspectives* 42: 224-246.

Talageri, S. 1993. *Aryan Invasion and Indian Nationalism*, Delhi: Voice of India.

——. 2000. *The Rigveda: A Historical Analysis*, Delhi: Aditya Prakashan.

Tewari, R. 2004. 'The Myth of Dense Forests and Human Occupation in the Ganga Plain', *Man and Environment* 29(2): 102-116.

Tripathi, Vibha. 2001. *The Age of Iron in South Asia, Legacy and Tradition*, Delhi: Aryan Books International.

Trautmann, T. 1997. *Aryans and British India*, Berkeley: University of California Press.

—— (ed.). 2005. *The Aryan Debate*, Delhi: Oxford University Press.

Vats, M.S. 1940. *Excavations at Harappa*, Delhi: Archaeological Survey of India.

Vidale, M. 2000. 'Review of "Colonial Indology. Sociopolitics of the Ancient Indian Past"', *East and West* 50 (1-4): 588-596.

Wheeler, R.E.M. 1959. *Early India and Pakistan*, London: Thames and Hudson.

——. 1968. *Flames over Persepolis: Turning Point in History*, London: Weidenfeld and Nicolson.

Winckelmann, S. 1994. 'Intercultural Relations Between Iran, Central Asia and Northwestern India in the Light of the Squatting Stone Sculptures from Mohenjodaro', in A. Parpola and P. Koskikallio (eds.), *South Asian Archaeology 1993*, Helsinki: Suomalainen Tiedeakatemia.

Wolpert, S. 1997 (5th ed.). *A New History of India*, New York: Oxford University Press.

Index